CW00428192

TO SEE THE SKY

VIGNETTES OF GRACE

2012

TO SEE THE SKY

VIGNETTES OF GRACE

Grace to you ~

with love ~

Judith

JUDITH HUGG

TATE PUBLISHING
AND ENTERPRISES, LLC

To See the Sky
Copyright © 2011 by Judith Hugg. All rights reserved.

The opinions expressed by the author are not necessarily those of Tate Publishing, LLC.

Published by Tate Publishing & Enterprises, LLC
127 E. Trade Center Terrace | Mustang, Oklahoma 73064 USA
1.888.361.9473 | www.tatepublishing.com

Tate Publishing is committed to excellence in the publishing industry. The company reflects the philosophy established by the founders, based on Psalm 68:11,
"The Lord gave the word and great was the company of those who published it."

A portion of the proceeds from "To See the Sky" will be donated to the Community Soup Kitchen in Morristown, New Jersey

Book design copyright © 2011 by Tate Publishing, LLC. All rights reserved.
Cover design by Leah LeFlore
Interior design by Nathan Harmony

Published in the United States of America

ISBN: 978-1-61346-519-6
1. Biography & Autobiography / Personal Memoirs
2. Religion / Christian Life / Inspirational
11.09.09

DEDICATION

To Tom, love of my life, sharer of skies.

TABLE OF CONTENTS

INTRODUCTION:
WHOM DO I LOVE?

I hear people talking about their radical, "first-love"-kind-of-wide-eyed love for Jesus, and I usually try to stay out of their way. Those people are a tad overzealous for me—like my friend who used to call God "Goddy" as her way of establishing how sweet their relationship was. Come on, folks; it's the Lord of the universe, not a Beach Boys surfer-summer-love thing. I very much believed in a Creator/God pretty much since I was born; there was always a sense of a being beyond myself who had the answers, who made all of this, who was caretaker to this great invention of planet Earth. I always had a sense that, in the coming of new seasons, the peace of flowing waters, the gift of a rainbow in the sky after a storm, the sound of voices of the people I love, that God was present and accounted for. I figured out as a teenager, when most teenagers were running screaming from their family's religious institutions, that God loved me and cared about me in a personal way and that my life, aligned with that love, was going to have meaning and purpose (along with those ubiquitous "learning experiences" that kept me on my spiritual toes).

But (I frequently argue with myself and rarely win) God himself *is* love; Christ was the human embodiment of that radical, wild love, who sacrificed his life for those he loved to death. This is not just an "I-love-my-SUV-with-7,000-miles-on-it-and-heated-seats," suburban kind of love, or an "I-love-(movie/television star name here)-because he's/she's-so-awesome," dismal-kind-of-hormonal love. This is the most stupendous reality on the planet: that we are connected in the deepest love-pledge of existence to the very heart of the God who created atoms, molecules, science, math, and music. He *is* love, he gives infinite love, he radiates love; he is trying to persuade the world of his love by loving the stuffing out of each one of us. So my love for him would be, well, I don't want to get too carried away here because of my denominational ties, which often get us labeled as "the frozen chosen." Whatever I would give back to him in love would be so miniscule as to be as insignificant as I feel when I look up on a cloudless, moonless night and see the layer of stars that I can see, knowing there are thousands more layers of lights and planets and molecules of stardust that I can't see.

Of course, I love God. But I realize and am willing to admit that my love for God is like my distant human love for a difficult person; I am determined to show love, I will care and be a positive, though inferior, resource for him, but my love is a little outside and to the left of the affection normally known as love. My love for God can be a bit aloof. It can be shy and conditional and disinclined to expression for fear of over-expressing. I want it to be like my love for someone fabulous: sparkling, freeing, wind-in-my-hair wild, but how do you get your arms that far around God? In what way do I love God? How do feeble human words wrap themselves around layers and layers of infinite love and grace?

Maybe if I wrote him a love note, telling him the places where I catch glimpses of him, how I am tickled by his fabulous artwork of cardinals, lilacs, and beagles—his expressions in the created world—how I struggle to know and understand his ways, how I will grab onto his eternal coattails and hang on for dear life no matter what. I could make the leap to convey, inarticulately, my love; to prove what is vulnerable scientifically; to put to words the inexpressible. I will reach out to him with the wounds that are deep and still painful to the touch, and I will see the love in his eyes and be still before his healing care.

So here I am. Here's my confused, clumsy, inefficient love note—my story of where and how I found God's grace and care along the way. Let the words of my keyboard and the meditations of my heart be acceptable in your sight, Lord.

MY FIELD OF GRACE

I can still disappear into my field. I can still wander to that long-lost place in my head—a huge field (maybe five acres, but it was my whole universe then) of tall grasses and wildflowers in the haze of a smoldering summer day on the dead-end street where we lived in the tiny town where cows would once in a while escape and be found wandering in the street, much to the consternation of our tiny local police force. The air is steamy to breathe, and warmth radiates from the ground, from the clumps of sweet-smelling grasses, from my freckled arms, and I think from the pure fact that I am a kid and have the whole blissful summer to burn.

I live in that crackly grass. I live there in the bitter sweetness of childhood summers. I pick flowers, make dandelion chains and bouquets of Queen Anne's lace and unknown pretty blossoms that quickly shrivel in the sun. We—my big brother and a small, sweaty band of neighbors with all their various dogs, plus

15

little me—dig up fabulous fossils and huge stones to build fort walls and find disgusting worms to horrify anyone near enough to horrify, usually of the feminine persuasion. When there are sudden, black thunderheads coming that darken our world, sometimes we can chase the storm in toward the house. We can hear it rumbling ominously closer and watch it slicing in sheets across the foothills like a giant monster dragging toward us. And we stand at the edge of the field, and the monster wall is almost on us. Then we race, yelling as we dash to our houses before it starts to flood and drench us. My brother can beat the storms in; he can run faster than Mercury on a good day. He has long legs and a fierce determination never to let his little sister win anything, ever. I get drenched, and he likes to lock the door behind him for a minute as I scream outside in the rain. If I ran as fast and got as excited and out-of-breath now as I did then, I would probably need CPR.

I play a pathetic game of baseball, "like a girl," with the neighbor kids in our field. My brother has tried forever to teach me to pitch a ball, and I have no control. My feelings are hurt to tears at least twice a day because I am the youngest of the crowd, always trying to keep up with my big brother, who would like it if the spacemen who left me years before would come back and take me back with them to planet Stupid. But the kids, the dogs, the field are all one wonderful organism, swaying in the breezes of sizzling summers in New Jersey, and we always play together on these vacation days before August starts to bring hints of fall and the wearing of shoes and the dreaded threat of school. The field only empties when the ice-cream truck ventures down our dead-end street or when parents yell for the fortieth time that we have to come in *now* when it's pitch dark out, and we then become contrite, filthy, obedient little angels and go home since we can't see much outside anymore anyway.

We managed every year to somehow be totally oblivious to the fact that there was an evil end to these sweet, mystical times, that the Thursday after Labor Day—it was *always* the Thursday after Labor Day in our town—would find us in new, crisp (soon to be not-so-crisp) clothes, sitting at a well-worn, wooden desk where someone had tried to sand off last year's initials and artwork, sweltering in uncomfortable, too-tight shoes. Sweltering barefoot in the field, free, wild kids hanging off trees like ripe fruit in July is such a different entity from sweltering in a September classroom, sitting up straight and still, the smell of bathroom disinfectant and new pencils and chalk dust instead of flowers and Pez® and fresh rain. Across the street from our house still lingered our beautiful, balmy field world. It became an after-school place for football and other games, but homework and responsibilities and the shorter days and increasing cold made the field mostly redundant the rest of the year. I wonder if it missed us, or if it misses us still.

I can, in the blessing of memory, set myself softly down in those crackly grasses and feel embraced and warm, even though across the street in our house the yelling and anger and complicated anguish of my parents' fuming marriage and my mother's dark illness never stopped. The field was a rare gift for my brother and me—a place of peace where I think I must've first experienced God and had the sense that we were not alone, that the beauty there could lessen the pain that waited across the street, and that the gift of beauty in that field was some communication of love and hope from someone beyond myself.

The field, which someone in later years declared so rudely to be "real estate" and on which strangers planted a large house, was the first place where God's voice started to be translated for me into a language I could understand. I didn't worship the flowers and the rain, but I literally rolled and reveled in the love I found there—the love of the one who created such beauty to cradle a sad, shy little girl and all her dysfunctional family and neighbors and friends. I secretly knew it was all from this God I'd heard rumors of, and that all good gifts were from him.

A PLACE FOR ME

I'm big on locale. I remember the people too, in broad, sweeping strokes from bits of my past, but the places form the structure of my heart. The house where I grew up and that field across the street were an extra set of much-needed limbs. The town where I spent the first seventeen years of my life comprises much of the cell structure of my brain. So many of the places in my life are now dead. The ranch-style house where I was brought when I was two days old was ultimately gutted and replaced by a two-story "modern" structure with bigger rooms and a gargantuan kitchen and all of the cold lack-of-charm that can make a house not a home. The open porch where my brother and I used to eat peanut butter and jelly sandwiches and play board games and evade mosquitoes on those steamy, endless summer kid days is long gone, replaced by a family room, just like the family room of the people next door and the people next door to that, with an

HD, flat-screen television and a sound system and electronic playthings. Okay, I'm making myself sound like an ancient relic here, but the playthings we had were each other, the rain that gushed off the clogged gutters, the ubiquitous deck of cards, and the neighbors who'd plod over to see what we were up to daily if we didn't get to their place first. I had my "good old days," and I'm sure my parents had "old days" that were even simpler and better than our "old days," which must've meant that my grandparents' "old days" were absolute paradise.

But I digress. My spaces were either havens or places of great torture and despair—secondary school was a good example of the latter. North Boulevard Elementary School still lives on in my heart as a haven, my first experience of school and a place of great successes for me, before the ravages of junior high and high school took all my "potential" and creativity and joy and jammed them into a testing and grading system that pinned me to the hallowed halls like an experimental bug with its tiny legs extended. North Boulevard School was where I learned all the really good stuff, kindergarten through fifth grade, and the rest of my education was a pale attempt to enhance said wisdom and knowledge. I had my first boyfriend there (we were engaged via a plastic diamond ring till he punched me in the stomach in fourth grade), cherished the annual book fair, was in the Easter Parade with aforementioned boyfriend onstage in front of the whole school (before public schools banned such politically incorrect apparently *Christian* institutions as bunnies and eggs and cute bonnets), had my first inkling that I wanted to be a writer—and never did master the monkey bars. I can still feel the coldness of the hallways, sitting on the floor with my coat over my head, waiting for the bomb to drop during what the newsmen called "the Cuban Missile Crisis." I can still smell the soap in the little sink that every classroom had and the chalk dust and the perfume my fourth-grade teacher wore. I still remember running my fingers along the primeval carvings of my predecessors in the wooden desks and seats. I remember Miss Paul singing to us and paying special attention with special love and attention to just me—and somehow to each child in her class—a rare art. I remember how peanut butter and jelly sandwiches used to taste—Skippy® and Welch's® and, yes, butter on Wonder Bread®—they've never tasted the same since North Boulevard.

I remember the place where I stood at the junior school when the teacher told me "I know just how you feel," in response to hearing that my mother had been hospitalized again. I remember that for the second time in my life, though I was usually as compliant and polite a child as you could've ever hoped to have, I yelled in despair at an adult and disputed what she was saying and stalked off in a rage. She had the good sense to let me go. I have never been able to hear anyone say "I know just how you feel" to anyone since then without wanting to explain with great vehemence that no one knows how anyone else feels, and it is the height of presumption and ignorance—and a rotten, unthinking thing to say to a suffering child.

I remember what a black-and-white soda tasted like at Ben's—Ben's, which was plastered with every advertisement known to humankind at that moment in history—on those rare summer evenings when we would go out as a family and hang out like all the other normal families, and I remember the sound of the pinball machines played by the Greasers at Ben's. Ben's was a newspaper/magazine/cigarette/soda shop, and I never knew if there was an actual Ben. But it didn't much matter because adults generally didn't have first names in my child mind anyway. But I remember those black-and-white sodas and rare summer evenings in our sleepy town where nothing much seemed to happen to anyone ever, and that wasn't a bad thing.

Jesus went to prepare a place for each one of us—some translations have it that "in his house are many mansions"—but I would settle for a lean-to in his presence, with occasions to catch his ear and to hear him speak and to have supper with him and maybe a black-and-white soda in the house of the Lord on some peaceful, eternal summer night.

RAISED BY WOLVES

My brother and I were raised by wolves. Padding through beautiful hills and fields, my cub brother and I skulked, searching for prey, happy for the cover of darkness, though not for sleep.

I have long since grown tall and learned to live among those who think they are normal, but on quiet nights, in the chill of a shadow or in a steamy haze at the end of a long summer day, I've still been known to bay at the moon. Some things heal; some things change, but the past never budges.

I wonder what will take me home eventually. Will I just remember it's over as I wake up one day to God, my heart having just given up its job to move to higher ground? That's the good hand we all want to be dealt by God. That's what we all say we want for the end. The rigors and humiliations of disease or extreme old age might polish my soul to the brightest of all the suns, but pain and the crucible are only desired by people who are fanatics. Wolves and regular humans like myself chase the slightly cushioned or faintly medicated way. We want to lie back under a crescent moon in the fields we love and wake up to the next reality with no suffering in between.

So I was an orphaned wolf cub, dirty and with matted hair, racing through the woods to the next drama, and then I suddenly came to the terrifying edge of the wood, and I was in college and was expected to speak softly and bathe and eat not only *like* humans but *with* other humans.

I recall my first Halloween out of the wild; I made a costume that dressed me to look like a garbage can. So many people saw that and saw the wolf in the scared girl, laughing off the garbage, but no one could get close enough to rescue her.

I took some time off from college and life to hide back in the trees, but it was too late, and they didn't shelter me anymore. I ventured to New Hampshire and then to Canada—and then to Ireland where I met a lovely, unkempt English wolf and married him a year later, and we lived happily ever after for several months, until I discovered that he was really a scared child and my really quite harmless growl could make him cower, and he left me for yet another species.

Wolves turn out to be meant for the pack and for the woods and the fields, but I was not enough of a wolf to rise to the level of my own incompleteness.

DEEP WATERS

On my seventeenth birthday, I saw the Atlantic Ocean for the first time. I've told people this, and they look at me strangely—they often do this anyway—because I grew up in New Jersey, which is actually rather close to the Atlantic Ocean; as a matter of fact, it sinks a little bit more *into* the Atlantic Ocean every time there's a major storm. The entire state is pretty much oceanfront property. But it took me till I was seventeen to finally stick my feet into its warm sand, artfully littered with shells, and fall totally in love henceforth and forevermore.

Our family had only one vacation when I was a child—not once a year, but *once*—an early summer disaster when I was eight. This trip involved driving great distances, roving north with two angry parents, one map (I believe it was of Lithuania), two kids, and a sizable collie dog in a 1958 Dodge something-or-other with a hole in the floor behind the driver's seat that my brother and I poked and picked at. We succeeded in enlarging it enough to throw things out onto the road to watch them disappear, cars swerving behind us to avoid our debris. We landed at some point—I don't know if it was intentional or if we were actually headed in the wrong direction—at West Point, where Dad took a series of pictures of his attractive, happy-looking family, seemingly without a care in the world. We were, at that point, only one month from my mother being hospitalized for six months in one of those state hospitals that adults speak of in whispers and kids make vicious jokes about. The camera lied.

But when I was seventeen, my mother's illness was on hold through medication. My brother had left home for college, then the US Air Force and marriage. I was leaving for college the following fall, and my father decided that this would be part of my birthday gift: the three of us—mother, father, and seventeen-year-old—would drive down to Sandy Hook. It was a rare epiphany in our family, a normal, sane moment when we could enjoy something together without any great drama. I wished my brother—and our beloved collie, who had died the month before—could've shared it with us.

It was a gloriously warm, October day. The beaches at Sandy Hook were basically deserted, and we spent hours walking and talking, collecting shells, musing as other people's dogs romped in the waves, each of us stopping, lagging behind the others, alone along the beach to just gaze out to sea. I remember seeing my father staring out at the waves. It felt odd to see him, for the first time in my life, in this different, peaceful, natural context. I remember thinking with some fear that he had feelings I would never know anything about, that there was a life this man had that was not my own and would always be unknown to me. I thought a lot about losing him when I was a teenager; I thought a lot about death. I loved Ray Bradbury, Edgar Allan Poe, and the gooey clocks of Salvador Dali and would probably have benefited from extensive counseling at that point, but in that era, it wasn't fashionable.

I was obviously not what might be considered a happy teenager (is there such a thing?), but that day I was free of myself, mostly ecstatically happy, feeling an instant connection as we came over the rise to see the ocean and the incredible vista of sky and sea to this incredible part of the planet I had only seen in pictures. The sky I'd watched from home matched so well at the horizon of this mountainous miracle of untamed power—the ocean. The hugeness of it was astonishing to me. It made me want to travel, to see the span of distances I'd never conceived of before. England was over there; Europe across there. That day, God cracked open the world for me. Maybe he had more for me than the home I had outgrown. I was a painfully late bloomer—certainly had miles to go beyond that day to reach any level of maturity. I hadn't even driven a car yet and didn't want to ever get my license for some reason or fear I can't remember now. I pathetically hadn't had a date, hadn't kissed a boy "for real" yet, never even went to a single school social function. But that day, really late in life for someone from New Jersey, I had finally seen the ocean and the possibilities of life beyond my very small world.

My husband and I go to Stone Harbor, farther down the New Jersey shore, every year now for my birthday. (People from New Jersey go "down the shore," a New Jersey expression that has never caught on in the rest of the country.) I take my Bible in the mornings and walk down to the beach and sit on the rocks on warm October days and listen, with God, to the waves and the spray and the armies of sandpipers and the Psalms and the hope of distances inconceivable, and I think of the journeys I have made and the travels I have yet to come. It is a thin place for me; in Celtic legend, the thin places on earth are places where God meets us head on, where heaven meets earth in more clarity than elsewhere, and I don't think I'm alone in looking at the wide expanse of ocean that way. Maybe because we are mostly made of water, the ocean can be a mystical meeting place between God and us. Maybe it's the rhythm, the sheer volume of it, or the total picture of sound, smell, and sight that overtakes all the senses at once. Or maybe it's just because God likes to hang out by the water too.

IN TOUCH WITH MY INNER RODENT

Perhaps the science of psychology will come up with a distinct warning about this phenomenon someday, but right now, analysis of imaginary playmates remains benign. My imaginary playmate when I was a child was Mousie. Mousie lived in the birch tree in the front yard, hibernated over the winters as my thoughts of him drowsed, and revived in the spring so he could keep lookout over our family and neighborhood from his top branches away from cats, parents, and reality, to warn us of impending doom, imminent danger, or if Uncle George was driving up the road for a surprise visit. I don't remember if Mousie had an actual voice; he just connected these things to me in our secret relationship until I was in second grade or so. (You were worried I was going to say high school, weren't you?) I know I loved Mousie, and I know that he filled various needs for me as the littlest kid in the neighborhood; he was always littler than me yet was my internal defense against the humiliation of the big kids of Orchard Road. Mousie knew things about nature that no one else did; he was infinitely wise. My dear brother, once or twice, came in from playing and plotting to overthrow the neighborhood and told me he'd killed Mousie in some showdown of manly will, but when I ran outside to the peaceful birch tree, Mousie was always fine and assured me there was nothing to worry about, that my brother couldn't really hurt him or me, but that my brother really needed some psychological help. Mousie, in some fashion, declared to me that my brother was just a jerk and his being a jerk made me better than him, and that was something I could live with.

I can still remember and feel what it was like to have this wise, ever-supportive, albeit quite miniscule champion in my life, ruler over all he and I surveyed, protector of little, lonesome girls. I was starting to form a belief in a higher power in the universe and was confusing the attributes I craved in the God I didn't know very well yet with an imaginary rodent in a tree, with clouds that peacefully traversed past my bitter house, with the rare person in my life who would acknowledge me with anything other than contempt.

Childhood memories are vivid of those who either contributed to the brokenness of my heart or those who participated in its salvation. Mice and men. And women.

There was a woman in our church's Vacation Bible School when I was eight—my mother was in the hospital all that summer, and my brother and I were emotionally shipwrecked with an irate father who worked most of the time and pawned us off on various relatives and neighbors during the days and some nights—and when I walked into the parish house of the church the first day, I was a lost little gypsy girl. My hair was undoubtedly uncombed and knotted (Dad tried but wasn't good with these things); I was probably dirty, sullen with grief and anger and fear. And this woman—probably a high school girl, but she seemed a hundred years old to me—put her hand on my shoulder and spoke to me, asking me my name and whether I wanted chocolate milk or regular. She smiled at me, asked me how old I was, asked me where I'd like to sit. She took my hand and led me over to a seat with some other kids who were doing a project and made sure I was engaged with them before she left me there. I remember looking back at her, and she still smiled at me. And she actually made sure I got chocolate milk. She listened to me. She heard me. She was my only encounter that summer with tenderness—a tenderness for which I was ravenous that summer; a tenderness I savor after forty-plus years. I didn't know about the words *grace* and *redemption* at the time—maybe they spoke about it at Vacation Bible School as I sat there wondering who'd be feeding us and who'd be putting us to bed that night. But this unnamed woman's sweet smile was my first encounter with the risen Christ, with the love of a God who reached out his hand with her hand to make me feel less alone. *Redemption* and *grace* were theological words I was years away from contemplating, but they were implanted in my heart for later use by this eternal gesture of one blessed, loving moment by one blessed, loving child of God who never knew what she had done, but whom I will love forever. I hope there is some provision for reunions with people like that in God's kingdom so that I could somehow let her know.

The birch tree in the front yard had to be removed because of disease when I went away to college. The woman in the parish house is probably retired from whatever she did by now, and she never knew what she did for me; I never even knew her name. But love is remembered. Anything that feeds a starving child is part of the good that is God. And all good gifts are from him.

A PRAYER AND
A RESCUE

On a gorgeous day in May of 1966, my suburban, pre-
sumed-safe world went dark. It was one of those days
when a thirteen-year-old girl should be allowed to walk
home from school slowly, lazily, obliviously, inhaling
the freshly warmed earth, the lilacs blooming in every
other yard, feeling the anticipation of good things after
the gray of winter, thinking about the boy in the third
desk who is *so* cute. And then my father drove up. My
father *never* picked me up from school because he was
never home until five thirty every night—5:30 p.m. for
forty years without fail, but here he was. And the door
opened, and he said something sadly nonsensical like,
"I'm picking you up today," and I went a little numb
around the edges. I dumped myself in the front seat
with my books and bag, and I could bring you today
to the exact spot on the street in my town, so vivid is

the memory, where Dad had to pull the car over again because he was suddenly sobbing so heavily that he couldn't see to drive. His shoulders heaved with the weight of the world, which was his lot in life at that moment. He told me that he had to take my mother to the hospital—again. She was sick—again. And then he fell apart again, weeping openly in front of his thirteen-year-old daughter from wounds I couldn't begin to understand and that we were never going to talk about on this side of eternity.

I remember looking out the window at my distorted world, shaking as my tough, usually stoic father sobbed. I was too shaken for tears and watching kids run by, trees moving in the soft spring breeze, other cars passing, bikes, people talking and laughing. I was frozen in a silent bewilderment—a painfully familiar one—wondering how it all kept moving, why they didn't stop in their ridiculous tracks, and didn't they know the world had just blown up and tragedy had just utterly drowned us and how could their world keep so merrily, stupidly spinning? But it kept spinning, and we went home after Dad's imparting of only basic need-to-know information about my mother: "She was taken to St. Joseph's Hospital this morning … We'll visit tonight … She's very tired and will probably just sleep for a while." It was bitterly familiar—okay, your world just got ripped out from under you again because your mother can't stay on the balance beam anymore, and you'll have to fend for yourself once again—at the age of thirteen.

We dutifully went to see her that night. How hospitals are supposed to be places of healing is beyond me: cinderblock walls, reminiscent of school, with splashes of pathetic attempts at too-cheerful colors, décor from a previous decade or possibly century, my small mother in a bed in a room with a window facing a brick wall, and no sunlight for miles. I remember sitting and reading *Life* magazine with the article about the new *Batman* television series as we waited for Dad, who went to talk to a doctor. My mother looked dead—or what I conceived of death as looking like—and the way she looked was very near the truth for her—and for her visitors. We said stilted words she couldn't hear, and then we quietly left, staying to the middle of the corridors to avoid some sort of magnetic pull toward the illness and the sense of hopelessness that emanated from each room and each blank face of each of the shuffling patients we passed.

Schizophrenia is a ghastly disease. It is relentless and howling, and it creates mutations out of some very sweet people. It can entail years of a normal life of work and family and activities of the supposedly sane, and then one day, you come home from school and there's a totally different woman masquerading as your mother. She mostly looks the same, but she says that someone is trying to murder her or there were mysterious phone calls that day or a strange man who smokes her brand of cigarettes has been standing out in the front yard by the maple tree. Schizophrenia is basically a mercilessly broken brain—broken by genetics or a prenatal injury or, in my mother's case, possibly the hit-and-run accident when she was a young teenager that crushed her skull. When she was put back together, including the insertion of a metal plate in place of her forehead, she was never the same. Maybe it was caused by a combination of factors, and it doesn't matter. There is no cure, though the medicines have improved over the years. She has experienced peaceful periods of a reasonable life, and then she had electric shock treatment back in the early sixties, when it was experimental and more torture than medical treatment. She's been a den mother and a resident of a state mental hospital. She spent one entire Christmas season sewing an entire wardrobe of Barbie doll clothes from fabric scraps for me because we couldn't afford the store-bought ones, and she's spent an entire summer under lock and key in a psych ward. Now that she is older, she can still hold a pleasant conversation, laughter included, but frequently she experiences what is called "word salad," where sentences are strewn together with off-the-wall words interwoven in place of regular words. ("I am fairly much strawberry today.") Word salad is such a nice-sounding concept. But it means that my mother's brain is not through shattering yet.

I remember the statue in the lobby of the Catholic hospital where they'd taken my mother. I've been to this hospital since then—it's the hospital where my father died twenty-four years later—and the statue is no longer there, but the cement walls and cheerless décor, updated but still behind by a decade or two, remain. I stood in front of the statue of Joseph holding the baby Jesus and was touched. Usually I saw representations of Mary holding Jesus, not Joseph, not the father with the baby. This baby, Jesus, as I remembered from Sunday school, had something to do with hope for the world, with strength, with the good-guy kind of power. I needed some of that. And I craved, though I clearly wasn't grasping even my own feelings at the time, someone to hold me, to hear me, to know me, to help me own what I was going through. I wasn't a baby, but I was thirteen, scared beyond understanding with the fear that my mother was "sick again."

On the way home, in the backseat of the dark car, the two main men on the island of my isolated little life—my father and my older brother—were in the front seat, not speaking. We were linked, sent into battle together again. The enemy hadn't yet been named; the word *schizophrenic* wouldn't be spoken in my family till after Dad died all those years later. And there on the front lines I said the first genuine prayer of my life inside my tired, confused head. It wasn't made up of words someone else wrote for me; it wasn't a prayer someone else had said as I obediently folded my hands in the Sunday school-prescribed manner, listening to them pray. It was my heart connecting with the God of the universe and with his Son—that baby who grew to be someone of love and power and hope for the world. I took a chance, took the plunge in the dark of the car, of my heart, of my young life. I asked this God, who I'd really only heard rumors of, to give me strength. That was it. Not "give me a sign," "send me to the deepest, darkest place in Africa to do your bidding," not the profound prayer found in the 900-page dusty book of some dusty theologian, but just "God, give me strength." What was different in my prayer that night was that I believed he would. I reached out to grab him with no doubt that he would take me in his arms and rescue my heart from the dark. It wasn't a bargain; it wasn't a one-shot deal. It was the beginning of a life deal, of a challenge. "You just be God, and I'll be a God follower. I'm empty; I have nothing left at the tender age of thirteen. Give me a life, and I'll live it. Fill me up, and I'll follow you anywhere." And he did.

HEAVEN

When I was a little girl, when there were big clouds—especially dark clouds before or after a storm—I would see a hole where shafts of light would come through, and I would think, *This is where God takes dead people's souls to heaven.* I don't know where this juicy bit of theology came from, but even now, when I catch this phenomenon in the clouds, it looks as though there's a porthole in the sky and maybe some action could be taking place between God up there and us down here. While I have grown and matured in my walk of faith, some views of heaven and God's presence and God's watching over me have never quite caught up. While I have grown and matured in my walk of faith, the bit of me that is four years old has remained behind, still staring straight up so as not to miss anything God might have to offer, which, of course, would come from up there.

Heaven, no matter what I read and what I hear, still seems like it's "up there." "Lift up your eyes unto the hills; from whence cometh your help?" seems to be saying that looking down at my feet isn't going to help in my recognition of divine intervention, but looking upward might give me a clue. "My help comes from God," by the way, is the answer; the help isn't actually emanating from any hills but from getting the focus off my toe fungus and onto an eternal power greater than myself.

At the Ascension, when Jesus went back home but left someone (the Holy Spirit of himself/of God) to remember him by, he rose up into the clouds—*up* somewhere to an actual place or dimension or planet from whence he will come back *down* someday. When he talks about watching for a sign, he uses the sky to illustrate how we know when the storm is coming, when the wind will rise. Our sky extends far beyond anything scientists have control over or can map completely. There's a lot happening up there.

It's a parade of fabulous white, gray, silver, pink, orange art that is never the same twice. It is a fireworks display unlike any other when the thunder starts to roar. I'm still learning to listen and see.

GLIDING TOWARD PENTECOST

During a sermon on Pentecost (which is the birth of the Church, not always much to do with the churches with the lowercased *C* that you have around town; I'm talking about the complete package, the body of believers, the real thing that clothes the hungry, comforts the thirsty, gives a cup of cold water to the sad and lonely in the name/love of Christ) our minister talked about the Spirit of God "knocking your socks off." (This is as opposed to the type of snore-inducing sermons that talk about the same old, same old, make the cross on which Christ died in passionate love for my rescue seem as tired as the carved, dusty, old cross on the communion table, and end with a loud, rousing "God be with You till We Meet Again" to test if the congregation is still conscious). My brain, in the mode of the spectacles of the Spirit of God, wandered back to a moment of letting go in my life.

My husband and I were vacationing in Vermont and saw an advertisement for glider rides at the local, very tiny airport. On a perfect fall day, we made reservations (I already had considerable reservations) and drove out to this diminutive destination hidden among fields and entirely too many tall trees to experience gliding for the first time. We entered a squat, odd-smelling building with what I remember looked like a World War II movie set. The pilot, a very nice-looking man, greeted us; he seemed to be a receptionist, taker of reservations and resident clown. I remember hoping that he would be more, well, serious.

We never saw the pilot for what I kept referring to as the "mothership." He seemed to be the one in charge of the "tower" and probably landscaping on the side as well. I decided to go first, trying to appear brave for absolutely no good reason I could think of, while really trying to get this adventure bravely over with. The clown-guy and I boarded this little glider, drooping on one wing in the grass. There was only room for him and me. I was strapped in to the front. I thought, though it was pointless to argue, that the *pilot* should be in the front, but these are trained professionals, after all. He got in the seat behind me, and I noted that the glider jostled and banged with every movement. It seemed entirely too fragile to transport humans. My brother and dad used to make those balsa wood planes that wouldn't last through a full day of play—I tried not to think about them too much.

My pilot explained everything that would and could happen and was quite jolly in telling me that he'd never been in a crash and never lost a passenger. The other pilot, the one on the plane that had actual engines, the one with the actual power and controls, also sounded quite jovial over the radio. My husband waved from the sidelines with an odd sort of grin, I thought, as my pilot gave me some instructions—none of which I remembered then or now—and then our little glider was being tugged from the weeds by the big plane with the actual engine very slowly.

I had a flashback within a flashback and remembered a cold morning a hundred years before when I was very young and I was being shoved on a sled by my brother. (His ominous last instructions from our parents before we had left the house were "look after your sister.") I remembered sitting back and hoping simply, in my total powerlessness, that older people knew what they were doing. I was skittering very fast down a hill near the local sandpit where one of the neighbor kids had broken his arm the week before. I seemed to have lived through it, which at the time engendered some minor and fleeting trust that my brother was an okay guy.

The glider, after thumping and bumping forward at increasing speed, actually left the ground—I remember being amazed, which was really quite silly considering that this was what we'd paid for. Then we were a few feet off the ground, then we were tree level (shouldn't we be moving further up, a little further, c'mon, just a little further), and then we were actually gliding behind the mothership. I could hear the comforting engines of the mothership—but nothing else. And then there was my pilot saying, "Here we go," though at that point, I was alive and therefore quite content the way we were. But despite my momentary state of joyful ease, quite suddenly, the mothership swooped a bit, and our glider dove a million yards with us to our death—or at least that was what my stomach and the adrenaline scorching my veins was telling me. Then the glider leveled off, and we were sailing with only the sound of air around us and the psychedelic broccoli of the autumn foliage below, the baby houses, and overly blue bodies of water that looked like they were snatched from my brother's train set. And we were slicing through air with just the gentle hand of God under and around us, and I felt such a bond of cloud and sky and self that I have never experienced before or since. I had to get past terror and ego and self-preservation to break through to this moment where I had no control over anything around me. I had no power, no responsibility, no tasks to accomplish, but what I had before me was this astounding view of the planet and of myself that so surprised me and overtook me. I felt free in every cell of my body, and it felt like I was always meant to feel. That's what happens when I can actually let go and let God do his thing and allow the cables (fear, the past, resentments) to be loosed and allow myself a faith freefall, to trust that I won't crash, burn, and die, and that there's actually more to life than gravity.

The heaving air sickness that began moments later is an unnecessary addendum to the story.

NICE VIEW

Here I stand, a rest on the way, my Agway some-what-toothless rake up against my chin, surveying our blessed October acres. The oaks are majestic—I actually own ancient, massive oaks in my yard, or rather they own me—as I pick up after their 150-year-old hides and watch the clouds and leaves swirling, defying my first-of-the-season efforts to clean up the yard. (Since it's a yard and garden, which is 99 percent dirt, why do we call it *clean*ing up?)

So it remains dirty and beautiful, and it's actually only about one-tenth of an acre, but it's ours and the bank's, and we love our little haven of sixteen years.

We have three bedrooms, a back porch like my parents' house had, a sunroom, which doesn't get any sun because of the towering oaks, and a garden with many varieties of non-blooming perennials. We have a dog, Sid, who followed in the paw prints of our dear mutt, Bear, who died two Septembers ago. Bear was ten, twelve, or possibly fourteen, depending on which vet we spoke with; the shelter people never knew, and it never really mattered. Now Bear is ageless, the stuff of suburban legend. Neighbors got to know us as "the people with the big, goofy dog, Bear." And now we have Sid.

Sid is a purebred beagle with traces of beagle blarney and entirely too much mascara. He is a canine food terrorist—a chow addict of the most obsessive sort. Sid is also a very spiritual sort, having started his life in a Jewish home and then being adopted into our Presbyterian home five years later. He gazes up at the sky longingly at times (communing with the angels? Begging the heavens for something other than cardboard for dog food?), cocks his head in recognition of our emotional state ("What are you, crazy?"), and looks very depressed when we leave for church without him on Sundays. (Or work on Mondays or the dry cleaners on Saturdays). He is a very centered, well-rounded beagle who has the doctrine—dare I say, dogma—of leisure honed to a science. This creation of God knows about "staying in the moment."

One day, Sid somehow managed to get to the center of the back of the kitchen table and drag an entire loaf of fresh-baked banana bread to its death. When

I arrived downstairs later after answering e-mails and puttering upstairs, all that remained was a mauled carcass of tinfoil and an uneven trail of crumbs into the dining room. He had dined in style, our beagle.

Over the next twenty hours or so, there was a series of unfortunate beagle emanations that we needn't document, except to say that rug cleaner is now on the grocery list again and I now know intimately the space behind the furnace, which has pretty much completely and blissfully eluded my thoughts of any housekeeping efforts these many years since we bought the house. (Why did he need to go back *there*?) And I thought the polyurethane on the hardwood floors would withstand pretty much any assault, but the floor company had obviously never met a beagle or his stomach acid before. Thank heavens for large potted plants.

Fortunately, we were having a warm January, and I was able to tie him up outside while I got some things done and let him urp with impunity for several hours. I kept watch, and after I let him in, he slept for the entire afternoon in a patch of sunlight on the loveseat in the living room. He occasionally looked up to glare at me, no doubt to thank me for my expertise in baking banana bread. I personally, after smelling used banana bread for most of the morning, don't ever want to bake one again, and I think Sid would agree. Meanwhile, the intended recipient does not know the fate of her banana bread to this day.

On our usual walk of the beagle before bedtime, my husband and I were wowed as we walked to the front of the house and saw the full moon just over the horizon, where it looked huge and surprising and gorgeous. We talked about what the night must look like on our dock in New Hampshire—our annual vacation rental from friends that we hearken back to in memory and long for during the year—which is set by a quiet lake and reflects the moon and the stars like a timeless mirror on still nights. Most nights, we point out satellites to each other and wait patiently for "shooters," sometimes seeing more than ten shooting stars a night. Sometimes we recline on the hard dock, freezing and tired, and only see satellites and hear the owls across the way. Two different years, we were rewarded with the otherworldly sky flames of the northern lights that danced for hours over us. We lingered long after the show, hoping for an encore. We are connoisseurs of skies, my husband and me.

Sid had some energy back by the evening—unfortunately, peaking just as we were trying to go to sleep. He wanted out, and since I'm not the one going to an office in the mornings nowadays, I rescued my husband and wrestled myself from sleep to go out with him. The temperature was in the forties, so I put on my long coat over my sleep shirt, slipped my dog-walking loafers on my icy feet, and took a very anxious dog out into the back garden.

The moon was tangled in the huge oak by the pond. Without my glasses on, it looked like a comet soaring. The air was clear; things are so quiet even in the suburbs late at night, and it was so odd in January standing in my backyard with no snow anywhere in the stillness. I watched the moon, and it watched the dog and me while I kept my eyes upward, having had enough of looking downward at the dog's self-inflicted trauma. *There are almost as many stars visible as there are in New Hampshire*, I thought. What a gift I have in the different skies I can inhabit, dream of, watch in awe as they change and dazzle me. I whispered, "Thank you, Lord," watching the moon watching us. God caught me in my backyard in my jammies walking a sick dog, thanking him for his creation and majesty. I do think he was pleased, if not amused.

I had to go walking in the garden three more times that early morning. The moon was haloed in clouds on the 4:00 a.m. watch, and I thanked God for how beautiful it all was and for his lights shining on our way again. The moon still has a sense of majesty to me, as it did when I was a child, and it is a shard of God's creation and reflects the sun's light so gloriously it can be blinding. That sense of awe from childhood—the sense that everything is fresh and new and unknown—still sneaks into my pedestrian, adult sensibilities sometimes. I thought about my life, invented as a reflector of God's light to a darkened world. The next morning, I was so tired I could've fallen asleep standing. But I had seen the moon bathed in its special light the night before, and it set my hand directly in the hand of God, and that's not bad for a saga that started with a liberated banana bread and a beagle.

DOG BYTE

Seed Pearl of Wisdom (Some Assembly Required)

I watched Sid the beagle watching a bee harvesting the foxglove blooms for almost ten minutes. I thought it was amusing that the dog could entertain himself by watching a flying bug gleaning goop from flowers. Then it dawned on me that I was amusing *myself* by watching a hairy, four-legged little oaf sitting in the warm grass watching the bug.

And a loving God is amused, watching us all.

SKIES OVER BUDAPEST

I have viewed clouds, rainbows, storms, lightning, shooting stars, *aurora borealis*, comets, and pure, clear-blue or grayish-blue or candy slices of the sun setting red in the following places (though not all in one trip): Budapest, San Diego, Liechtenstein, New Jersey, New York, the north and south of Ireland, England, New England, Scotland, Wales, Findlay, Ohio, France, Germany, Switzerland, Washington, DC, Pennsylvania, and bits of Canada. The clearest, most persistent rainbows were in the south of Ireland, hands down. The most shooting stars I have seen at one time were, oddly, in the clear skies over Morristown, New Jersey, during a dawn Perseids meteor shower. The most phenomenal sunset color palette to make me gasp was in New Hampshire. The smallest sky is in Liechtenstein—but it is of good quality. The brightest lights obscuring the sky are in the city of New York, in my experience—and in the state of New York, I seem to have spent much of my time quite depressed for reasons having nothing to do with looking up to the sky and much to do with looking down, literally and spiritually. Though I remember a quiet lake on my sole lifetime camping trip where the stars reflected in the still water, and I felt like God could come and sit down and laugh and have a beer with me. I stopped drinking soon after that.

I think it sounds the most interesting that I have been in Hungary, the country where my mother's parents were born (though with quite different borders) in the 1890s. Both John Freedman and Mary Greenbaum came through Ellis Island in the beginning of the twentieth century, looking for safety, freedom, and those gold-paved streets. They met in New York City, married there, and had their two children in Brooklyn before moving to New Jersey for reasons that are obscure. Freedman and Greenbaum—well, they weren't Presbyterians. I love that Jewish root system I have and still light the Sabbath candle and say the prayers in their honor and loving memory. Grandma died when I was eight; Grandpa John Freed (as they changed his name at Ellis Island) lived to be 104. We often attributed his longevity to his roots in the Carpathian Mountains and to the fact that we never saw him during a full moon.

Hungary is a beautiful, very bruised country. When my husband and I were there in 1996, it was just beginning to make slow progress toward political stability and economic strength. I was fascinated with some of the lectures we received on our tour, comparing them to stories my grandfather had told of the old country and the multitudes of upheavals. I was basically looking for my grandparents everywhere—in the faces of the people in the streets, in their hair color, the sounds of their words, the gold-flecked hazel eyes. I was breathing their air, seeing some of the same sights in the countryside and cities and towns of Hungary that they saw. We had a boat ride along the Danube—even Grandpa had said it was never blue—and I have never felt closer to those two people, two people who, by reason of grief, culture, and emotional distance, I never really got to know by heart. When I looked at the mountains, maybe I was seeing what they saw when they were young, when they had their whole lives ahead of them, when they dreamt of what was to be.

There is always an element of surprise to me that when I arrive in a different country, the sky, the dirt, the shops, the hills, the people, the trees all look essentially the same. But there is so much I can't conceive of in the differences of culture, experience, time, history, and perceptions. Did I grasp a sense of Mary and John and my own roots and branches and heart, or did I miss them altogether?

Part of my story, my history, my heart started in those skies, in the deep forests, by the waters of the Carpathian Mountains in the nineteenth century. I have connections to God there by family, by blood, by some memories of Grandma and Grandpa, who spoke differently from everyone I knew but who sounded like home to me.

SKYWRITING

No one seems to know if it was a summer, spring, fall, or winter phenomenon when that "Star of Wonder" guided the Magi from the East and shepherds from the hills and perhaps other similarly nameless people to find God's not-so-secret hiding place among humanity's poor stuck away in a barn with the animals and the hay and the dirt. There was an obviously spectacular astronomical happening that was the backdrop for heaven and nature singing—angels coming out of hiding to raise the roof because the promised Christ was finally shedding this new light on the world, lowly though his beginnings seemed to be to those who expected otherwise. There was no turning back, folks. The curtain was rising, the show had begun, and there was already a standing ovation that could be heard across the universe for one baby born among the donkeys and rats and stars.

Sky was also featured prominently when it seemed as though his light had gone out. The earth shook; there was darkness over the earth as his Spirit left, as his body was given over to death. The darkness of the evil of his torture and departure matched the darkness of the world that he had just left.

And then, three days later, there was this sunrise. It did not jive with the darkness of hopeless mourning that so many felt. There was light, and there was an angel directing traffic away from the tomb, from death, from hopelessness. God loves light. At the creation, he called it good. He nicknamed his son, Light. This day was all light. There was light dawning on a new, miraculous resurrection. There was light dawning on the faces of the women who came to the garden dreading the sight of death but who found the light of life. There was light from the angel declaring the most unbelievable thing: he who was dead is alive. There was light beginning to come to the travelers on the road to Emmaus who walked with the resurrected Christ and thought they saw something in him, but, no, it couldn't be.

When Christ comes again, he will come from a sky near you triumphantly to claim his royal inheritance—his imperfect children who reached out to him in faith and hope. We probably won't need a star or angels doing harmonies or big storms or anything. We'll know him this time.

MY FAVORITE ROOF

For eleven years I worked for the Sisters of Charity at their retirement residence down the hill from their college. I did their medical bills and insurance claims. But, as you hopefully can see, I am a writer, so eleven years of accounts and Medicare claims and signing off on bills was not exactly what I saw as being my highest calling in life, noble a job though it may have been. But I needed a job at the time, and I came to fall in love with the sisters there. The residents and staff and visitors were a riot of odd characters and memorable scenes, and this world of the religious and their convent was the stuff of legend to me—frequently pretty funny legends, especially for a lifelong Protestant. There was one legendary sister, now long gone, who was for many years in a wheelchair and would signal with her hand one who she wanted very much to speak with. In earnestness, she'd beckon that person with her ancient, bony index finger, indicating to him to come closer and closer so she could tell him something very privately, and when he was right up to her face, ready to hear her prayer request or her blessing—she'd punch him in the face. Many a new nursing assistant was introduced to the world of the sisters this way. I was grateful for the warning before I succumbed to her bidding.

The building that housed these elderly sisters was an early twentieth century white elephant, solid as the Rockies but infinitely impractical as a nursing home. The rooms were "cells" as the sisters were used to, but when I worked there, they were years away from being up to code as the nursing home they aspired to be. Thus the place was referred to as their "retirement residence." (Later renovations have solved that status and ruined the merry white elephant forever. Such is progress, to be practical but reduce any charm or quirkiness to dull development.) The cells were plain with one chair, one dresser, one cabinet big enough for an extra habit and a winter coat, and they all shared bathrooms. The bathrooms were made of literally tons of white marble, which, after almost one hundred years of scrubbing and dings from wheelchairs and wear, was singularly unattractive. There were three floors of these un-air-conditioned residential cells, a fourth floor for live-in sister staff and visitors where the elevator stopped, and a totally wasted fifth floor, jammed with ancient walkers, canes, wheelchairs, and perhaps some old sisters who'd gone missing over the decades. There were stairs too steep for any of these elderly ladies to have ever climbed from the fifth floor to the tar roof, which had a door with *two* broken locks.

I remember when someone from the housekeeping staff first took me on a tour of this ancient building; the last stop was the roof. (It was rumored there was a swimming pool up there, which someone has managed to convince new staff members of since the seventies.) We were not supposed to go up there, and we had to be careful, as there was a fairly low ledge around the perimeter and nothing to stop us from unceremoniously plummeting six floors to the parking lot below. The fact that it was forbidden and dangerous made it my favorite hiding place for eleven years. When the boss was being humiliating, which was standard operating procedure (when I left, probably three-fourths of the administrative staff, including myself, were premenopausal, which left quite a mark on the place), or worse, when I would come in on a

Monday morning and find that one of the sweeter sisters there had passed away during the weekend, I would go up on the roof and muse for a while and sometimes—well, frequently—have a good cry.

On the Fourth of July one year, my husband, Tom, and his mother and I came in the front door (that lock didn't work either) of the building around dusk, took the elevator to the fourth floor, and trudged to the roof without anyone seeing us. (Such was their level of security at the time.) It was a gorgeous, cool night, and from the horizon began sparks that seconds later would thunder in the sky. Within minutes, the whole horizon was bubbling and exploding with firework displays from every town within fifty miles. We *oohed* and *aahed* through the next hour, surrounded by exploding wild stars and cascading rainbows. We three were about twelve years old between us, excited at the sparkling sights and sounds around us. There were a lot of world worries at the time, and I was only one year orphaned from my father. But up on the roof, the world was fresh and alive. The show was magnificent; we hated to see it end, and we made our way back down the steep steps through cobwebs to make our way home again.

SHOWERS OF BLESSINGS AND TEARS

I've given and attended a number of baby showers in my time, usually for relatively well-to-do, traditional mothers and babies-to-be, and somehow I thought this was another same-as-the-others party with pink lemonade, pink whipped cream on the strawberry shortcake, pink carnations and pink begonias in a cup for each guest. It was to be a nice surprise for this special mom; it would be Katherine's introduction to the neighbors, and it would be a blessedly joyful and celebratory night. I had the venue worked out but forgot, as I frequently do, that I am not in charge of the outcomes in life, and an unseen hand can make wild, enchanting fireworks out of the smallest spark.

Katherine was adopted from China. And after two years of working with agencies and authorities between New Jersey and China, my dear neighbor friend and her husband had brought this beautiful little girl home to our neighborhood. Katherine was small for her age—already eight months old when she arrived—and she had health issues and was statistically behind in the growth curve for her age, but she would get past this quickly with the love of her parents and her new neighbors and some decent nutrition and care.

Everyone assembled on schedule in the pouring rain on our covered back porch—I love when that works out—and then Katherine and her parents arrived, happy and incredulous at their surprise party. Everyone touched and snuggled Katherine in blessing and welcome. Then our recently widowed elderly neighbor swam over in his green raincoat and ancient umbrella, holding something in a bag very close to his chest.

What he brought was an antique wooden music box, a replica of his wife's hope chest from sixty-three years before. It had been a gift to his wife after their first son was born. It played Brahm's "Lullaby," and he wanted his newest neighbor to have it—to pass it on to the coming generation. We listened to this music that Katherine's ears had probably never experienced—a sweet moment and a generosity that moved everyone there.

The strawberries and pink whipped cream and candy kisses gave way to gift opening: outfits, bonnets, a photo album, crocheted blankets, a tote bag with Katherine's name, and one googly-eyed stuffed cow with a bell. The sun was going down, not that we'd seen much of it anyway in the deluge, when Moira, a super-mom of three, gave a blessing that hushed everyone and tied a bow around the proceedings. I thought I was giving the surprise party, but I managed to get that happily wrong.

She took Katherine's face in her hands—Katherine seemed quite attentive, I thought—and told her, "Little girl, you have no idea yet how much your mommy and daddy pleaded with God to have you in their arms, how much you are loved, how much you are wanted here. I pray you know how precious you are to God, to Mommy and Daddy, and to us. We love you, honey." There was never a finer sermon said in any church. Our porch had become holy ground. There was a deep silence from us all for a moment with the harmony of steady rain, intermingled with some tears. Mostly mine. I give good parties.

NO FLAMMABLE
SHRUBS IN SIGHT

Okay, I've never "seen" God. At least, I've never experienced God like Jesus experienced his Father's literal indwelling presence, like Moses was acquainted with God's voice and persuasion, or like the disciples saw God directly via his Son, Jesus. I've never seen Australia either, though I've heard reports and seen things that come from there (kangaroos, Paul Hogan), and it all makes me pretty confident that there probably actually is an Australia, and I'd even like to see it up close and personal someday, minus the gigantic poisonous spiders and Paul Hogan.

I can't offer any scientific or conclusive academic proof on the existence of either, though photos taken of Australia pretty much make a substantial case (and there are people who've allegedly been there who've filed reports), and stories, secular and sacred, of a creation epic and writings on the existence of things beyond our understanding are a good start toward saying hello to a concept of a real God.

Post-modern people have wanted to push the whole God/miracle/mystery thing out of the way for quite some time, assuming the mention of God meant that someone was going to start strong-arming them, preaching at them to do what they said (which is, of course, what God said), or they'd be sent to a place of fire and brimstone, which may or not be somewhere in California, which is where they've calculated Christ will return on the 16th of December, next year, sometime after lunch. Actual God stuff, the outward trappings of some of the modern church (televangelists, stewardship campaigns, the blessing of circus animals in the sanctuary, hair and fashion from the previous decade—or century—and music from the previous decade [or century], ministers who are against Halloween, Christmas lights, and anyone ever having even touched a Bible with the Apocryphal books *in* it) *can* be very irritating. But they are off the subject of the actual Creator of the universe who has peppered and spiced said universe with stories, pictures, puzzles, gems of himself, waiting for us to say, "Oh!" and light bulbs to form over our thick heads.

On the other hand, some "modern" people have made their concept of God into such a fuzzy-wuzzy buddy concept, or such a mystical, composite, new-age, God-is-everywhere-in-everyone, cannot-be-distinguished-by-religion-because-He-is-too-too-universal, watered-down version that any God wishing to speak would be drowned out by his own ambiguity.

But about this God thing. I've always had a sense since I can remember that he/she was there. When I was a teen, I spoke my first actual prayer to him in the aftermath of a family crisis, in the back of my father's car, driving home from a hospital. For the first time, I could articulate it; I knew suddenly that night that he was personally involved with me and that we could touch and know each other closely. He answered and is still answering that first prayer from my heart to his, as well as many others since.

When I first heard Edvard Grieg's "The Last Spring" at a music appreciation course in high school and tears raced from my heart to my eyes, I knew that sense of there being more to this life than just the outward appearance—the stuff and nonsense of my routine and pulse. If nothing else, the fact that I'm alive and a fully, albeit oddly,

functioning human being at this juncture is definitive proof to those who've known me for some time
that "there must be a God." And some of them
even say they've been to Australia.

THROUGH THE
NIGHT

I daresay the sun probably came up pretty much in the usual way on Saturday, April 28, 1990. I don't remember much about the day except my husband and I drove to my parents' house for a sort-of belated Easter dinner and celebration and my mother gave me a stuffed toy owl, which for unknown reasons we named Ozzie. Everything at the house on Orchard Road was as it had been since I was brought there when I was two days old and my brother told my parents to take me back because I was too small to play with. (I'm not sure that the house had actually been cleaned with any vigor since those days either.) The drive back to our apartment was uneventful; I was making egg salad for dinner because we'd had a big lunch—and then, the world suddenly blew up, and nothing was ever going to be the same again.

So many life changes I've heard of begin with a phone call. In the movies, there's ominous music, then a silence, a look of horror, agony, that sudden loss of control that sends the character shivering from a well-ordered day to sudden, irrevocable emotional chaos with the simple answering of a phone. Mine began with words from my mother, which are tattooed on my eardrums: "I think your father has had a heart attack."

I have wild, ragged shards of memory from that evening. We raced back to the town where I grew up, to the hospital named after the man who brought my brother and me into the world, not knowing if my father was alive or—the unthinkable. Hadn't I just hugged him good-bye a couple of hours before? He was always a great hugger. He said he hadn't been feeling well. He'd probably call the doctor Monday; please call the doctor Monday, Dad. In our race to town, I was in a flood of tears, husband Tom trying to console me, to assure himself and me, meanwhile praying he wasn't lying. When he left me off in front of the hospital so he could find a parking space, I flew into the emergency room. I found my mother in the busy ER waiting room; she said Dad was alive, but no one had told her much more. A very kind hospital volunteer ushered us to the doctor, who was blessedly very compassionate and smart in dealing with families, but he kept saying things from a soap opera: "He may not last the night"; "the situation is very grave"; "everything possible is being done." He assured us that Dad was comfortable, and yes, we could go in and see him, but just for a moment, and every hour he lived was a positive step toward recovery. I called my brother, and we calmly spoke of when he would be able to arrive from Pennsylvania. We spoke dispassionately about what the situation was. Then I called a friend, and though I wouldn't do it talking to my brother, I broke down in a fresh flood of tears on the phone with her and begged her to pray—of course, begging my Father God to let my father live.

We finally got in to see my father, who had fought in North Africa in World War II, who had built three-fourths of the house on Orchard Road with his own hands and considerable sweat, who had survived scarlet fever and rheumatic fever as a small child—plus a whiff of phosgene gas during the war. He had survived two children, the death of his own parents, the series of crises with a sick wife. And there he was, kept ticking with tubes and wires and beeping machines all about, and my father looked terrified beyond what I thought I or he could bear. My tough, strong, angry dad was foreign to the role of helpless individual. And the three of us (my brother would arrive the next morning) did what we always did to cheer him and each other up, to make nice out of a bad situation, to make whatever pain there was go away: we made stupid jokes. We berated Dad for making us drive all this way again; we made Dad laugh, and then he seemed to relax a little, and we told him we loved him and were praying for him and he owed us a croquet game when he got out of this mess and that he'd better get out of this mess as soon as possible.

Then the doctor told us to go home and wait. Tom took me back to that house on Orchard Road where I grew up, and he went back to our home to make some phone calls, to get some rest, to come back the next day with clothes and TLC for me. The house where I knew the creak of every floorboard, where my brother and I had been conceived, where nothing ever changed was changed to be so off-kilter that I felt an evil closing in on it I'd never sensed before.

When I got to the house, there was a foot-long gash in the sheetrock outside my brother's old bedroom from where the gurney had made the turn to take Dad out in the ambulance via the front door. I thought about finding plaster, painting it to make it right that night, to erase the horror of it, to somehow make it not have happened. My mother made tea, and we sat at the kitchen table as we had done centuries before—Dad's empty place at the table to my left a yawning chasm. I don't have any idea what we talked about, but it was an adult conversation—two women hurting and powerless beyond what we'd ever experienced in our lives before. I thought about all the times Mom and I had had tea together in that spot since I was a child. She used to make us both sweet tea, and she would iron and talk to me in peaceful times. Now we were at war against time and the ravages thereof, ravages that were trying to take my father. There was that familiar feeling of the house again being a battleground, the unspoken war raging again without our consent.

I thought about that phone ringing. I willed it not to ring, because a phone ringing meant inconceivably bad news. With every hour he lived, there was more hope, the doctor had said. Hope can be fierce; I always thought of it as a gentle gift, but now it was a roaring lion.

I finally collapsed onto my childhood bed in my old lilac-colored bedroom, no clue what time it was, and it didn't matter. I knew sleep wasn't likely to come, but I needed to cry alone and to pray and to try to find some peace side by side with my fears. Faith and fear are often in the same room together, and they were not battling, just keeping me company. I kept trying to say the 23rd Psalm over and over, but in my numbness, the words kept getting jumbled, fleeing, eluding me. I would hear my mother get on the phone to call the hospital to hear if we were still together, if she still had a husband, if I still had my father. And through the night we were still a family, we were still hanging on. I'd come out into the kitchen when I heard my mother, and she would give me the report. We would hug, and I would go back to pretending that sleep was a possibility, back to my old purple room with the Beatles posters still inside the closet. Dad had built that closet, that room, that part of the house. Dad was strong. How could he be lying in a hospital bed, separated from us, from his house, flirting with death, so weak that death could flirt with him?

He lived through those fragile hours that night and many nights after. My brother and sister-in-law and their son arrived that next morning, and we took our turns in the ICU with Dad, and the demon of the threat had passed. We were a bit too eager to sweep it under the rug, but Dad was alive, and everything else on earth was a distant millionth in line for things that mattered. God had brought him through. Our prayers were answered. God had given us a reprieve. God had resurrected the dead. And the fact that perhaps God gave us this gift to prepare us for the four more months we had left to say our real and final good-byes to Dad would've been too much to endure in those first days, so God, in his mercy, kept that from us. Because having scarlet fever and rheumatic fever, a heart murmur from childhood, a whiff of phosgene gas in the war, and diabetes has to lead somewhere, and that somewhere is not usually in the longevity category.

On September 8, 1990, after a four-month struggle with congestive heart failure, more hospital stays, and finally, the quadruple bypass from hell performed by a doctor who greeted the family before the surgery with bloodstained shoes and coat and a declaration that there was not any hope, my father died having never regained consciousness after the anesthesia. My last words to Dad—and his last words to me—on my phone in the office at the retirement residence where I worked, were "I love you." I could not allow myself to think that it would be our last words spoken on earth. I could only have hope, though the doctor said there was no hope, which no one should ever again on this earth be allowed to tell another person. If you ever tell it to me under any circumstances that I have no reason or right to hope, to live in hope, to go to God with hope, you'll be in dire need of painkillers soon after.

God answered our prayers during those last moments of Dad's life in September with *no*. God let it all shatter around me, and I felt during those days and the brittle, painful days to follow that he made me walk through all the broken pieces barefoot. I always believed, and still believe, that God is present for me and for all of us, that God is love in many different ways, and that God isn't capable of deserting his children. But as I looked in the usual places that late summer and early fall for his comfort, for his strength, for what I always knew of him, there were the deepest clouds descending, and I couldn't find God anywhere.

THE END

She was waiting for him with her arms folded.

"I refuse to believe in the existence of a God who permits the suffering of innocent children."

"So why are we getting married in a church?"

"To melt his heart," she replied.'"

—From *The Constant Gardener*,
John Le Carré, page 259

A twenty-year-old man committed suicide on a recent Monday night. He jumped out from behind the signal box that is about 200 yards behind our garage, right into the path of a train going sixty miles per hour. I heard the train stop suddenly on Monday night—it parked behind our neighborhood for over an hour—and I quickly heard the police sirens and wondered what had happened. We read about it in the paper the next day.

At the back of our garage there is no siding as there is around the rest of the house; someone had conserved money there many years ago, and we've left it that way. It is bare wood, and when we first moved in, I painted big letters on the old wood in brick-red paint for everyone in the trains to see: "Travel Light," and I painted a big cross underneath. Friends have commented when they go by on the train or on the bike path parallel to it that they have no trouble figuring out which house is our house. I wondered if this young man saw my silly message on the back of my garage. I wonder, as he planned this devastation to himself and his family, if anything of God went through his mind. What level of pain must he have been in to have made that decision to jump in front of a speeding train, to endure that moment of agony for the freedom from the agony inside, whatever that entailed?

I've been listening to the trains go by for the last few days, thinking about the life that was obliterated so violently on that night behind our house. I've known pain in my life, have considered what purpose the pain, grief, tears had in my life and what possible purpose I had in the world and with God. Some years ago it could've been me contemplating an end—any end—to the deep aching that nothing would relieve. Divorce sent me there; rejections from those I deeply trusted made all of life look horribly pointless. It frightens me that someone could be so selfish/brave/cowardly/hopeless to derail his own life. It frightens me because living this life can sometimes be utterly unbearable, and despite popular belief, it doesn't say anywhere in the Bible that God doesn't give us more than we can handle. God allows for the most horrendous suffering; he set a world in motion that kills us all eventually and wears us down year by year in the process. He let his Son endure the searing agony of the Roman torture of crucifixion. There is an eternal purpose to suffering, and God doesn't say I'm exempt.

But he also gives grace and hope and the occasional picture of our lives, disengaged from the natural laws of the universe, in communion with him beyond the world's psychoses, in greener pastures. His name is Jesus, who suffered the agonies of the death of a parent (Joseph seems to have left the picture fairly early), rejection by his peers, his friends, the disciples (the New Testament version of the Keystone Kops—what a crowd to have to work with), the very culture that he was born into, and a hideous, degrading, vicious, drawn-out death on a cross.

I couldn't trust a Savior, I couldn't buy into a God with my whole being, who would've done anything less than that for our tender human hearts.

TWO HUNDRED
BOXES

Up in our attic are 200 boxes of dynamite. No, we're
not really harboring explosives—Homeland Security,
please note. It's the emotional explosive that hides in
the recesses of my mind, and the 200 boxes from my
parents' house from when my brother and I closed
it down and shut the door for the last time in 1993.
There are boxes of books—mine and my father's
and mother's—and there are boxes of uninteresting
kitchen implements and pedestrian pots and pans;
and there are boxes with mines, blasting caps, cherry
bombs, old family photos I haven't seen since Dad
died, documents from my grandparents and their nat-
uralization papers when they came to the New World,
my grandfather's divorce papers from his second, very
brief marriage, drawings by my baby nephew—now
thirty-three—that were done in the previous century.

And there are the stories my mother wrote, stories she submitted to every inappropriate magazine known to mankind about her daughter's pregnancy (that's me, and it was never true), a perfect happy family, her life caring for horses—all manufactured by the devastating illness of schizophrenia. And though I know it's a disease for which she is blameless, her way of living with that disease continues to put a stranglehold on bits of my life and keeps so many childhood memories boxed in with shades of gray. And many of those shades and shadows and bits and pieces are literally lurking in the boxes in my attic.

We've lived in our home with the cluttered, crowded attic for a lot of years now, and for reasons of a need for more storage and the fact that it's all becoming a fire hazard, it became time to face the boxes. Maybe it was because the trails through the boxes, along with the paths through the boxes of our own stuff, were shrinking more and more urgently until it became harder to scythe our way through the underbrush to find the Christmas lights each year. Maybe it's because Tom gives me "the look" whenever he struggles his way up there to find something. It was partly because I was determined to find the

New Testament my father brought with him through North Africa during World War II, and it used to be on my shelf of Bibles and reference books, and it mysteriously disappeared when we moved to this house. Or maybe it was just time, plus the fact that I was really afraid that someday the ceilings would collapse on us as we slept.

I'm afraid of having memories evoked that have been laid to rest up in those boxes. I'm afraid of my own feelings becoming demons as they rise up and shake off the attic dust. I don't want to be re-engaged with them again. They are painful, or rather, they were.

I need, more than accessing more storage space, to face down the memories. Grief that had power over me ten years ago doesn't necessarily have that kind of power today. It would be better to just open the box and let some fresh air in. My parents are gone, the house is gone, childhood is over. I wonder what is in those boxes that is stunting my growth even now. Better to find out one box at a time.

As soon as I finish cleaning out the boxes in the basement.

MOMENTS OF OCTOBER

My fiftieth year on earth was a very different kind of adult year for me. It was the first one in thirty years when I hadn't worked outside the home, full-time for someone. It was the first time I had the time to knit more than one scarf. I was barefoot more times this year than I was in shoes probably since my first year on earth—and barefoot is better. I read more books my fiftieth year, donated more blood and platelets, bought less junk that I didn't need anyway—which in previous years wouldn't have stopped me. And before my fiftieth birthday party, I had the blessing of spending time by a gorgeous pond surrounded by pines and red, gold, and wine-colored trees, wondering if I was happy and what the meaning was of all of the days God has given me.

It was a sunny weekend in October in upper New York State, taking a short holiday with a close friend. I was healthy, warm, entirely too well fed, lounging in a serene fall paradise. But I was still capable of feeling angst over issues at home (of which, blissfully, there aren't many right now), the possibility of my country going to war for oil or something, my burgeoning weight and cholesterol levels, the three gray hairs I found this year (but who's counting?). I had two days of this retreat to look forward to: quiet times of prayer and meditation, favorite foods, books, videos, walks by the pond, sunsets whose colors rival the fall foliage, that first sip of coffee on cold mornings before I get the wood stove blazing. Then I get to go home to a husband who loves me, a beagle who tolerates my impositions so cutely, a neighborhood and church full of good friends, and a party the next Friday at one of our favorite restaurants for a surprisingly large number of my favorite people who love me.

My brother has a kidney stone and can't come to the party; I pray for him, for his comfort, till it, well, passes. But he doesn't believe in "assigning human traits to the natural laws that govern the universe," and I wonder how the connection works when I pray to my loving God, who is unknown to the one for whom I pray.

It blossomed into a gorgeous day: a strong cold monsoon was blowing this morning, followed by quick clearing to a striking blue sky and fast-dashing clouds of cirrus and mare's tail—just lovely. And I sat, debating under the fabulous sky what I will wear to the party on Friday, and noticed the polish on my left big toe is chipping.

As I sat on the dock on that peaceful gift of a morning, gazing at mist playing with mist, watching the sun warm shades of wine, cranberry, pumpkin, sage, lime, and lemon in the hills, I prayed around my bundle at home—and thought about how stupid my socks looked with the holes in them (through which I could see my big toe, polish chipping).

The pines across the way were perfect pillars. One had lost branches to within ten feet or so of the top where there sat one perfect Christmas tree. The breeze toys with the mist.

And I started to wonder how the Yankees felt when they blew the playoffs last week.

I have the idea that when I was a child I was capable of being utterly single-minded and absorbed in the glory of God's creative works like two lovers drinking in each other's words, eyes, gestures, together-moments. But now the lovers have been married a few years, and they both snore, and they've traveled every inch of each other so many times that the road has developed some potholes, to hideously mix some metaphors. At some point, when I was about twelve, I thought I felt something mystical leaving me, some ability to see and perceive that I wanted to run back for, but a door had been closed that I couldn't jimmy open no matter how hard I tried. I remember sitting on the living room floor on a Christmas morning back then and thinking that things didn't feel the same as they used to, and the pure joy and holiness of moments was being filled in and was drowning with questions and anxiety and confusion. A shroud had come over my childlike heart, and I couldn't remember anymore what things used to feel like. I was grieving something I couldn't even recall. It was something to do with growing up, but it didn't feel like anything "up."

I want to learn to see again. I want to see beyond the pretty trees to being fully engaged in the moment at this place of holiness and peace. I want to hear the levels of gorgeous, delicious silence, a breeze, chipmunks chattering, the geese slicing through the fall air, making me feel separated from anything else that is noisy or financial or has to fit on a schedule, and grateful and hopeful because that moment is all there is right now to my life. When I stand over those candles on any given birthday cake, I want to be fully wings-spread, heart-unbroken, eye-popping alive and aware that the moment is eternal, that God is in it, that I am fully his, and that he is undoubtedly present.

But I scheduled a pedicure and got my hair done and fussed toward an impossible perfection first.

HAVING WORDS
WITH MY MOTHER-
IN-LAW

I don't take committee assignments, and I've never become an elder in my church—this is just not my calling in life, and I don't feel I play well enough with others—but one of the things I love to be asked to do is to assist with the Ash Wednesday services. I'm not good at the whole Lenten focus; Easter happened, and it is my life and hope, but the forty days leading up to it, I'm never quite focused well enough to follow a daily devotional booklet or a list of Bible readings in some sort of order. (Advent is even harder, but Lent seems more vital to prepare for, and I always feel like I've missed it.) But Ash Wednesday, I get it.

Since the Protestants gently succumbed to the Ash Wednesday symbolism, my Lenten understanding has increased dramatically. "Remember, from dust you came, and to dust you shall return." That is life at its most humbling. From the movie stars to the lowly freelance writer, from the corporate moguls to the women and men who actually do the work around the world, there you are. All we need is a Savior in between to make it all worthwhile. There's Easter. The eggs and bunnies thing I don't get, but I get the dust.

Life's short—and very dusty along the way.

My mother-in-law was coming to the service. She's been through two major surgeries (and a couple of minor ones) in the last year, and I've seen more and more the fragility of her life, and I don't want to say those words to her. She is a beautiful, dignified woman who has been through some of the most awful things in life (losing her husband and her father in the space of one year, as examples, plus having to bring up two rambunctious boys as a single mom) and has come through it all with a testimony of grace. She got her AARP membership a lot of years ago, and her years on this earth are statistically pretty much numbered—and I don't want to think about that. She's been in my life and heart for a long time, and the thought of her leaving us is sadder than I want to deal with. But she is dust like we are all dust. I like the idea that God loves each one of us like there was only one of us, like we were all beautiful, dignified children who all had his complete attention. If I'm going to assist in a service and declare us all dust, I have to accept the reality of her mortality, my mortality, the dusty mortality of every loving one who comes to my side of the chapel to receive ashes and hear the Word. It is a hard thing to look each person in the eye, like looking Jesus himself in the eye, and saying we're all from the same soil. We all need to be reminded so we can treasure every moment God gives us. Like that moment on Easter morning when we realize that we all have hope—hope is all we have, and dust is not the winner.

JUST ROUTINE

We were up and down the stairs, busying ourselves like most weekdays. I went out and switched the cars in the driveway so my car could get out first, skipping my coat and regretting it, teeth chattering by the time I got back inside, and in between, we were making the most infantile jokes possible about colonoscopies. I had my premiere colonoscopy some months before and had endured the stupid jokes—all the banter back and forth to calm the nerves and lighten the mood as we always do—and now it was payback time.

We drove to the huge medical building I've driven past a thousand times—a massive, white box with some very serious-looking people in the elevators who didn't look like they would ever joke about anything, ever. Now we were at the reception area, signing papers, making bright, witty repartee with the woman behind the desk, who had heard all the clever comments too many times yet managed to keep a kind smile on her face. Then we went to sit and wait, my picking out a comfy place for our jackets, my magazines and ubiquitous cup of coffee.

A woman in blue scrubs called out "Thomas," and my throat tightened up just a little. He got up to follow the blue lady and then said to her, "Wait just one second." He stepped back toward me to kiss me. No jokes. He walked away, all his stuff left behind with me, and I finally gathered the courage to say the words to myself: "This is a test for cancer." We are in our fifties; things can start to happen. Now we are starting to have cancer tests. What if…but I don't dwell on it. I focused my heart on his kiss and the loveliness of twenty-plus years together and the fact that God brought us this far. It was just a routine test. A couple walked up the hall looking ashen, eyes to the floor, coming from the room that Tom had disappeared into. We are over fifty now. Things happen.

A friend of many of my friends, who is only sixty-three (that used to be very old in my perception not so long ago), a health nut, a vitamin pusher, skinny as she was when I worked with her thirty years ago. She had a massive stroke recently. Who knows what will happen? We are all praying, but in my heart, God is just this side of a negligent father to take her down like that. She's never been married; all she's done is work for decades to support an apartment and feed a series of cats and cars. Not that she's had a bad life, but she has no family around, no one to take care of her, which someone will need to do now that she's paralyzed and may never speak. Sixty-three years old. Things are happening too fast. God loves us and takes care of us. It's a nice concept that maybe God doesn't give us more than we can handle. But sometimes, suddenly, we are given more than any three people could possibly handle in several lifetimes. Another friend who's been a good Christian girl, has lost three husbands to terrible illnesses—and now her present husband is ill, in a wheelchair for the rest of his life. I have no doubt that God's there. God watches. And sometimes, terrible things happen, and then they are compounded, and then they deteriorate from there. And then they get really, really bad.

It's hard to be somewhere in between that battle: to know that a loving God is present and that sometimes he will do nothing to step in and override the nightmare, and that ghastly things happen to the just and the unjust. My being a person of faith, hope, and love does not immunize me from the horrors this world can dish out like the Halloween candy with razor blades in it. God watches. God cares. God loves. But sometimes that love feels like total abandonment. His eyes of compassion can sear through innocent lives like an atomic blast. Then the well-meaning say, "God will never desert you." And you say, "Maybe I wish he would; all this love is killing me." And then you wait. You gaze at your very own charred landscape and try to talk to the God of the universe. The silence can be crucifying.

People come to this place to find out if they have cancer, to find out if the next couple of years of their lives must be spent learning more than they could've possibly ever wanted to know about chemotherapy and radiation therapy, and how tumors metastasize despite the best medical efforts, and some people will learn a language they never wanted to hear, with pain they never could've imagined, and a prognosis that decimates the most heartfelt and desperate prayers any church, synagogue, mosque, family, or single person alone could've dispersed to the outer reaches of the universe. God's there, but you can't touch him, feel his presence, see him, hear him. You can't have his deliverance just now. You simply have to do what you have to do.

My thoughts were interrupted by someone walking over to me who looked like maybe a college kid, doing janitorial work to pay for school. He's dressed ready to go outside into the cold day; he's in a big hurry, and he's coming to talk to me. Of course, he's the doctor. The Doogie Howser image gets stuck in my head. Thus I didn't rise to the occasion to ask questions till he was off and running. But everything went fine. Everything is normal. Thomas should come back in five years for a re-check. My throat tightens up just a little again. I was told I could leave with Tom in about fifteen minutes.

Everything's all right. It's not our turn yet. God is good. God would still be good if Doogie had told me that "we found something." None of this will ever be easy to fathom, but I will keep trusting our God of love, regardless. I've watched him taking care of my heart before, and I'll keep trusting that he's consistent with me, that he's not anxious to steamroll over my hopes and loves. And if I choose not to trust God, what would be my alternative?

WHY ME?

Peggy died eleven years ago. She lived up the hall from me at college and had the best sense of the ridiculous about people that I had ever seen up to that point in my life. This was important to me as I was trying to develop a fledgling system of understanding people at eighteen—kind of a mental filing system really of high maintenance and low, pleasant and skunky, gets me/doesn't get me—and Peggy gave me permission to laugh merrily at some of my evaluations, many of which would need to be obliterated later in life if I was to endure in society and not become the female unibomber—or a mama grizzly. Peggy could read people like no one I knew, and though as she matured she became kinder, as a college student, she had no patience for stuffy people. She would flit around them like a gnat, disturbing their funky sourness and then moving on quickly to other venues before anyone could get angry with her. She had a charm about her and an ability to escape conflict quickly. She could flit with the best of them. And she was my friend. She got me, and she made me laugh. And it was one of the finest affirmations to me as a young waif that I could make her laugh till she literally fell down.

The years screeched by after college, as they are prone to do. Most of us got married, got jobs, stayed in touch the best we could. Then Peggy developed breast cancer. She was doing well; the prognosis was good, but then the cancer was found in her bones. We cried and prayed and prayed some more. The cancer went to her brain. She was gone in less than two years. She left behind an adoring husband and three small children who suffered profoundly with her through her illness and beyond. She was a woman of deep faith and tremendous humor and even more tremendous love. She died young, reinventing the very essence of the word *tragedy*.

After my fiftieth birthday, I discovered a lump under my arm. I had been faithful about my mammograms and diligent about protecting my health, and thoughts of Peggy emerged almost immediately when I rubbed at this lump. I was scared. I called the doctor as soon as the offices opened on the next business day. I was examined. I was sent for an ultrasound. I walked into that office, vulnerable and shaken, sitting with other women in a waiting room of similar fears. I was brought to a back room and was told to take everything off on top and put on one of those thin robes that assure you insights into humility previously not considered. I hopped up onto a pre-frozen metal table in my attractive, thin little fashion statement. The woman put the cold, slimy wand on the spot where I'd found the lump and raked it up and down and around like she was looking for a baby in there. She pressed keys on the computer, pressed the wand into my armpit. Nothing hurt except the thought of what happened to Peggy, what happens to thousands of women—and men—when cancer is found. The technician ended her exam and told me to wait for the doctor. Those three minutes of waiting were approximately twenty-seven hours long. The doctor came in and examined the area, mouthed the traditional doctor "hmm" sounds, and finally said those sweet words: "I don't see any irregular tissue on the ultrasound, and there doesn't seem to be any irregularity here. It may have just been swelling from an infection..." or something. Nothing to worry about. I'm healthy as three horses. For right now, at least, I'm free.

I left feeling incredibly strong and wealthy and prayed for Peggy's kids again and for all the others who lost part of their hearts to the plague of cancer. I get to leave the doctor's office with the "healthy" stamp. And I have to ask, "Why me?"

REMEMBER ME

I make the frequent mistake of looking too admiringly at some of my friends whom I consider to be the newly minted Mother Theresas of this century, and I regret that I am not as totally sold out for Christ—or for anything—as they are. They are the ones who do it all, who visit the poor and sick on a daily basis, who give until they are devastated with exhaustion—and then they find more to give, and they give more.

Comparison and regret are stupid exercises. I look at others and look at their upbringings, their circumstances, the gifts they get to work with, and to compare what they do and who they are with myself is such an exercise in futility. Yet I wake up the next day and find myself in the regret game again. They are so spiritual, and I am such a dog returning to her own vomit. (Aren't the Psalms just the bees' knees?) They have the strength of God to give tirelessly, to love the utterly unlovable, to minister to the sick, the hungry, the dying, while I am sitting on the couch eating cheese curls and watching *M*A*S*H** reruns. They never flail or flounder. They never yell at their pets, chew nails, eat an entire bag of chocolate-covered caramels at one sitting, or whine over the weather. These are righteous dudes. They shine like the brightest stars in the firmament. And compared to them, I'm in deep trouble on the righteous/goodness scale.

But God says I'm his child. I'm worth something, and if I'm worth something in God's eyes, then I'm worth quite a lot. I'm in his heart, on his mind, and not entirely damned just because I'm a snack food addict or just because I'm me. "There is none that doeth good—no, not one" pretty much translates to "Nobody's perfect." We are all in the same boat, and Jesus is calling us all to leap out of that boat and walk on that water toward him, and there's room in his arms for us all. Even Mother Theresa admitted to faults and doubts. She's my sister, somewhere beyond the clouds, and there's room for her and me and everyone who reaches out and asks this Jesus to "remember me when you come into your kingdom."

WOULDN'T IT
BE NICE?

Everything I originally learned about human love, I learned from the Beach Boys. And the Beatles. And a little from some of the other British groups from the sixties, though not generally the Rolling Stones. The Beach Boys actually had a song about how nice it would be that "we could be married, and then we'd be happy," and "maybe if we think and wish and hope and pray, it might come true; baby, then there wouldn't be a single thing we couldn't do." Oh, and then there was "round, round, git around; I git around," but that was mostly lost on me in the innocence of my teenage years.

One of my favorite songs from one of my favorite groups was "Do You Believe in Magic" by the Lovin' Spoonful about that "magic in a young girl's heart." I was the young girl with that magic and hoped there was a boy who would spark that magic. We would somehow find each other someday and know, from across a crowded room, that the other was *the* soul mate of my desires and dreams. We would be married, I guess instantaneously, and live happily ever after and do this relationship thing right because, of course, our parents never got the hang of it because they were decrepit and over thirty, but we knew about the real magic, and we would walk off into the sunset, supremely happy and fulfilled. That magic was supposed to free my soul, and no one else would comprehend it, but I would know its joy and, well, magic.

After a multitude, or maybe it just felt that way, of soul-deadening relationships with many depressing and depressive men of the tri-state region—one man who left me for another man, one who went off and got another woman pregnant because I wasn't ready for the level of relationship he wanted, and one who, on a chilly Valentine's Day evening, sat me on his knee and, with tenderness in his eyes, gently declared to me that he was in love with someone else and was going to ask her to marry him—I found out that real, live love bears as much relationship to the so-called love songs of my youth as Sid resembles the Taj Mahal. My heart was smashed into near nothingness so many times I was ready for a transplant. I eventually gave up on relationships with men for a while to get my heart and soul ready to be a woman alone, to be totally independent, to regroup, as it were, and finally picture myself as an important self without someone to "complete me." I was God's woman, dependent solely on him for the love and care I needed. My soul was finally free. I stewed sullenly in that little rant for a while. No, really, I knew that I needed to get alone with God and be just me and him and learn better to love and care for myself, but there was always a tremendous desire to share it all with someone who fit into the "love of my life" class. So I learned. I got much better at being me. I really had stopped looking at that point and expecting a man to make up for what I felt I was lacking.

About six months after my shaky declaration of independence, I met a guy named Tom. I saw him across a crowded room at a church function. He saw me, and I saw him and, surrounded by about fifty other people, we were alone together. Sparks flew. We drifted toward each other on the warm wings of an early fall evening. And twenty years later, I know what real man/woman love is. It's not just making those vows, as Tom and I did three years after our enchanted evening, but living them, sticking by them through death in the family, through illnesses, depressions, disappointments, diametrically opposed, utterly irreconcilable disagreements where I am totally correct—and, for heaven's sake, menopause. It's looking forward to growing old together, knowing our ability to remember where we put such-and-such is already getting a little flaky around the edges, our bodies are not what they used to be, and his hearing is lessening while my body fat is increasing. That honey-pie-baby-love gets old and develops wrinkles and a paunch (male and female) and liver spots eventually, no matter how much promise the plastic surgeon might offer. I believe in the magic. It's not Hollywood. It's the kind of stuff God had in mind when he invented marriage. Maybe we make God laugh. Meanwhile, we'll dance until morning.

THE HOUSE ON ORCHARD ROAD

I went into the town where I grew up to see the funeral director of the funeral home that will one day oversee my mother's funeral, though my mother is still very much alive. People do this nowadays to sock the family money away before the fact so that when the funeral is called for, there will be a reserve there for that purpose. It's part of "estate planning," an irrevocable trust to protect assets. It's called sensible. And it's one of the most macabre things you'll ever have to do.

It was May and already as hot as August, and I actually quietly said a polite and heartfelt "thank you" to my car's air conditioning before I got out of the car to go into the office. I stepped out into a full-blown New Jersey heat wave and felt like all the air had been sucked off the planet, or at least from New Jersey. I am very familiar with this funeral home; my brother and I used to play in their parking lot as children, and Charlie, the director, organized my father's and my grandfather's funerals. I thought of asking him after my grandfather's service if he gave group rates but didn't want to push his pleasantness too far. Charlie really was a very nice guy.

Charlie was as kind as I remembered him—I don't see how he could stay in that same family business with such a good reputation without having huge reserves of compassion and cool—and I was comforted to walk inside and be greeted by air conditioning that was running really well and by a sweet, old, drooly Labrador retriever who sniffed me as I walked in and then followed me to the office. She sat by me, and I petted her at uncomfortable intervals ("what year did we do your father's funeral service," and "make sure you get four copies of your mother's death certificate") and the old dear (the lab, that is) seemed to also understand and be skilled in the art of comfort and support. I signed multitudes of papers, read only some of them, was eager to leave, took notes on things I knew I'd never remember, and was proud of myself to have succeeded in this adult endeavor—and beamed out of there as soon as I could.

And then I thought, after having visited my Dad's gravesite, gone to the local sports shop/toy store that used to be our grocery store when I was a child, and wandered through the town, *Why not finish off this emotional bouillabaisse and go directly to the old house on Orchard Road for a good old, melancholic rush of memory lane, shot-in-the-head, family nostalgia?*

I'd driven over there many times over the years since I'd closed that familiar door to the house for the last time. The new people had put in a bay window, shored up the garage, updated the landscaping (aka, ripping out all the lilacs and the ancient willow we used to climb) and put up kiddie swings and fortresses and a high fence over the years. But this trip, I drove slowly past the old house on the dead end, and there was a gutted structure barely recognizable.

They were putting a second floor on the original ranch-style house. The roof was gone; a blue tarp covered the whole place. I pulled over, emboldened by shock and feeling like I was seeing a beloved family pet being bullied. I walked past a mega-Dumpster in our old unpaved, stone and dirt driveway and walked into the garage, which was, mercifully, a few degrees cooler. There were workmen working not hard at all; as a matter of fact, they were quite content to sit it out on this steaming day, and one chap told me I could look around. He really didn't seem to care if I removed a load of lumber, bricks, and supplies, as long as I didn't require him to have to move.

The couple who had bought the place had moved out; the entire house was a skeleton, and I could barely find my precious way around. This was a place I could've run through blind most of my life. I knew every inch, every corner, every creak, and every hiding place. Now there were no appliances—no walls—no clearly defined rooms anymore. Where my brother's room used to be, there was now a staircase. I wanted to scream against the disorientation, and I inspected like someone looking through a bombed-out area of a beloved city for the first time. The living room, distinguished originally by the fireplace where we had hung our Christmas stockings for a hundred years, where a cardinal had flown down and I had freed him years ago, where my brother and I would heat our backs until they sustained second-degree burns just to see who could endure the heat the longest, had been made redundant. There were bricks hanging off the border of it, waiting for final demolition. And they were building a new fireplace—a modern one with tile around it and a larger firebox, and I was trying to figure out how they would move the chimney and why they would have to mess so much with the structure of a house. Our old fireplace, the site of probably half of our childhood photos ("Smile. C'mon, *smile now*, or I'll give you something to smile about!"), was partly hacked out and was obviously a goner. I took pieces of brick and stone like taking seeds from an autumn plant before the frost, and it felt like someone was doing the wrong surgery on the wrong patient, removing the heart instead of the tumor. The builders had broken out the walls from my parents' old bedroom, my old bedroom and part of the hallway.

My parents had this ranch-style house built on an old orchard in 1949 right before they were married. Yes, it desperately needed upgrading, and I don't begrudge the second owners doing whatever they needed to do for their presumably growing family. But it is just hilarious and awful what needs to be done in the world to be "modern" and comfortable and up-to-date, to the point of losing an entire history. When we reluctantly sold this young couple the house ten years before, my brother and I presented them with a framed photo of the original home right after it was completed, before my father had made his own additions and adjustments. They seemed genuinely interested and lovingly placed the picture on the mantle over the now-condemned fireplace.

To see my childhood home become someone else's childhood home is as confusing as calculus to me. I view my reaction to it from that odd distance we take when things get too confusing. I am not quite sure what is happening, except that I am working on the accepting process that the world is not all mine to preside over and the world may not have the great and wondrous *me* as its main focus. Growing up, being able to face the hard work of adult life with grace and faith, is a surprisingly huge, ongoing process. When I was a child and spoke as a child, I assumed that when I graduated from college (which I didn't) or when I got married (which I did, twice) or when I had my first child (which will never happen), that I would suddenly, somehow, out-of-the-blue, be a "grownup." It never occurred to me that when God hardwired me as a human being to grow up to be this woman that my growing-up years were pretty much *all* of my years.

NEW FIELDS

I take the beagle for his long walk in the mornings, after prayer, breakfast, and ablutions, so that we can both lose weight, so that we can get out of the house, so that we can see neighbors and not hide from the world. And I've found a new field not far away where there is the same garden of Queen Anne's Lace and chicory and thistles and "bread and butter" flowers that I had as a child when I picked raggedy little weed bouquets for my mother that I viewed as worthy of a royal wedding. And there are wild blackberries to savor in season and a huge tumble of honeysuckle that adds a sweet layer of perfume over the warm air. I still pick bouquets of Queen Anne's Lace, not for craft projects of scrapbooking or anything else except to let them shed pollen on my living room coffee table and to look wild and gorgeous for a few days until I decide to go out and pick more.

Beagleboy leads the way. I let him wander, and I follow him, and sometimes he'll roll hilariously, gloriously reveling in some dry grasses while I'm choosing my flower arrangement for the day. We find golf balls and leave them by the fence posts for Arnold Palmer or whoever comes to use them after we go home. They always mysteriously disappear, and we find sometimes the same ones or new ones in the grass. (This feels oddly similar to leaving cookies and milk for Santa.) We've seen wild turkeys, bunnies, crows, small children running—just running for the sake of running, with no agenda, no direction, no time constraints. Sometimes he and I run too, although, if I'm holding the leash and he stops to smell a previous dog's roses, there's trouble and possible whiplash. I'd forgotten what it's like to run, to just run up a hill and down the other side for the sheer pleasure of running up and down and here and there with my dog and feeling the wind in my hair and my heart pound with the pounding of my feet. It is just not the same as the tedious buzzing treadmill in the basement by any stretch of the imagination.

I have had the incredible, luxurious privilege of taking a year off from outside work after turning fifty—after thirty years of jobs that were bill-paying, insurance-covering, 401-K contributing jobs with no reason other than the aforementioned cash flow. I just had jobs—no career—I did freelance writing to satisfy my real life. It is, of course, harder on us financially, but I feel free this year to write and breathe and find myself out from under the rubble of the jobs that paid the bills and deadened my soul. And I feel like I've been waiting for myself for thirty years to break out, to be a little more frugal, less clock-oriented, less living in a chronic forced smile with people with whom I was thrown together in an office, some of whom will be dear friends for life, some of whom should no more be pretending to supervise people than should Charles Manson. They are the reason Scott Adams (creator of the cartoon "Dilbert") is a bazillionaire— a man who was in the right place at the right time, laid off from Pac-Bell in the right era to start creating fabulous satire about the corporate world and its minions and victims. Some of the people who are my previous coworkers I've suspected he spied on at our staff meetings. I wonder how he found us.

My new field is only about ten minutes from the previous office where I worked with some of the most difficult employment demons for two blistering years. My new field is eons, light years, galaxies from that place. I can be Judith. I can be unprofessional, child-like, creative, occasionally un-showered, and no one on the planet is going to misinterpret the real me in a performance evaluation. *Nanner, nanner.*

I first found God in a field. I can assume that he also dwells in offices, factories, camps, skyscrapers, mines, stores, libraries, churches, synagogues, mosques, tenements, trains, villages, and possibly the halls of Congress—at least, sometimes. But the thin places on earth, those places where God is most accessible and surprising, I find to be places under a large sky. Flowers help. A nice warm breeze adds to the ambiance. Sometimes his best love is found in a foxhole, in a hospital, by a grave with my family name on it and flowers wet with tears. But anywhere he can be found, or where I can be free enough to see him, is a taste of home. Home is a place, a dimension, a dwelling where God is, and nothing else will matter.

A CHAIN OF TEARS

Our church has a prayer chain, probably like most churches do. Nowadays, they're done by e-mail, which is better than playing the phone tag game we used to do, when messages would get ridiculously mixed up. (My favorite was the *nun*'s pregnant daughter who was ill—it turned out to be the combination of several different messages.) There are some days when we have good news about a surgery that went well, a drama resolved, a test whose result was the blessed word *benign*. But most days, it's bad news. This one suddenly has a hideous, aggressive cancer. That one received news that her cousin was in a tragic, grisly accident. Or a major pillar of the church dies suddenly. We get the news first. Sometimes I don't want to get that news anymore. If I hear of one more victim of the vicious plague of cancer, I think I will scream. Oh, that's right, it's not about me. But it's hard to hear about more and more and more.

It's risky business praying for people—saying that I believe in prayer and then explaining to myself why one more report of "inoperable tumor" makes me crazy. It is hard on one's faith to face that next request and say, "God, I know you can do it all; you can heal one more." Sometimes a person is healed and comes back to us to thank us for our presence with them in prayer. Sometimes people require a long-term prayer commitment of patience. And sometimes they die. Most of the time, I don't know what to do with that fact in my life of faith. The puzzle pieces sometimes don't fit well.

I don't have a good, eloquent, one-size-fits-all answer about that. My answer is to keep praying; to keep storming the gates of heaven on behalf of other souls who don't have the energy to pray anymore because their life force is sapped by the demon chemotherapy. I keep asking and pushing and requesting and hoping, and people who are prayed for live or die or keep going however they're going; it's not up to me. I also don't think the answer is always that funeral favorite to throw in the face of the widow: "It was God's will." It is *not* God's will—God's best, God's loving hand—that someone loses a child after a year of excruciating cancer treatments, that a loving wife of fifty years loses a husband suddenly and has no idea how to cope alone. It is life, and it's the way it goes—eventually we all die, returning to the dust and all that. But as far as I can tell, God doesn't plot out gruesome ends for some and peaceful ends for others on some eternal whim. The world brings about murders, cancers (largely because of the mess we've made of our fragile environment), and the ubiquitous accidents by car, plane, icy steps, bikes, electrical sockets, sudden storms, etc. God set a planet in motion, and he doesn't mess with his own laws of nature. Except sometimes. I don't understand why some are healed, some are healed and then get sick again, why we all die the way we do anyway.

I will just keep praying because to *not* pray, to not connect with God, is not an option for my heart in an imploding world. As I connect and listen and rail and implore, I learn a little better that God is bigger than anyone or anything I can imagine, that I don't order him around with my magnificently worded prayers, and that if I were the one to be allowed to make it all happen, the world would be a giant tomb.

LOOSE ENDS

It really is a fast process, especially if you use fat needles and thick yarn. I've been knitting since I was small—my Hungarian grandmother and my mother taught me the basics somewhere along the line—and somehow, I don't remember the frustrations there must have been in the inevitable dropped stitches, uneven rows, and baggy loose ends of a beginner knitter. I don't pearl, and I don't increase or decrease (we are not referring to weight or John chapter ten here); I just knit. I knit great, long rectangles (scarves) and wider rectangles (baby blankets) and occasional squares (not much). I have lost count of the number of scarves I've knitted for people over the years. I may refine the art of geometric perfection in knitting someday.

When we drove to Pennsylvania for Thanksgiving, I brought my knitting. I had wanted to give my mother a new red scarf before the winter weather set in to go with the new red jacket she didn't know she was getting yet for her birthday, and I was running out of time. It was about a third of the way finished when we left. When we pulled into my brother's driveway, I was done.

My hands were stiff (aren't I too young for that?), and everything but the fringe—if she wanted fringe—was complete. I looked at my stitches, nowadays quite even and tight, and there were dog hairs knitted into the fabric from the beagle we'd left behind. There were stretch marks from transport; they would even out with a washing. Every stitch of it was mine; every loop in it was a motion of mine, assembling my mother's scarf. Made of red yarn, beagle hair, love, and crumbs from lunch, it was something special, completed on Thanksgiving Day. It is intricate, yet it is so simple.

It is a thing made of love. Psalm 139:13 says that I was "knitted together in my mother's womb," which scares me sometimes because of the genetic proclivities lurking in that womb, but then it goes on to say that I am "fearfully and wonderfully made," and that God knows what he's doing when he's working on us. What, ultimately, am I afraid of?

SOLEMN RECORDS

I somehow inherited a wonderful yet badly beaten, beige "records" book from Grandma Hugg, my father's mother. The first penciled entries in it are from the summer of 1922. My father, her second of six children, was less than a year old.

The book itself has printed tables and lists to help farmers and farmers' wives figure out antidotes for poisons (flour, water, and "mucilaginous drinks" if you happened to have ingested carbolic acid; I would check with my doctor before trying this at home), the quantity of seed required to plant an acre (five pounds of parsnips, in drills, two and a half feet, for those of you who were wondering), domestic weights and measures and legal weights/pounds per bushel for coal, corn, and Timothy and Hungarian Seed, among others.

The last president listed is William Howard Taft, whose inauguration was in 1909, so I can assume that Grandma got her records book on sale, as it was already a little dated in 1923.

Besides being a charming reminder of a time long past, the book contains a lot of memories of my family. It is another world to read about my father, born at only six pounds on Christmas Eve, and how he sat up, laughed aloud, and played with his hands (I don't know if that was all at once) at three months. My father took his first steps on May 21, 1923. He had six teeth when he did it.

In June of 1922, my grandmother canned eleven pints of large red cherries, fifteen pints of pineapple, five pints of pitted cherries (not the large red ones?), eight pints of preserved cherries, three quarts of peas, two pints of beet greens, more cherries, spiced beets, huckleberries, and then by August, there was corn to can and peaches and lima beans, etc. I personally wouldn't know the first thing about what to do with a lima bean—I won't even eat them—but Grandma grew up on a farm, and this must've all been second nature to her, learned at her mother's kitchen table. She canned and preserved and cooked and baked and took care of six children through scarlet fever, rheumatic fever, and one through polio. Grandma never drove a car and said that if she ever got as high as you get in a jet plane that she'd just keep on going to heaven. A practical, fabulous woman, my grandma Hugg.

There are a couple of pages devoted to church committees and who was bringing refreshments to the Christian Endeavor meetings (some of those yummy canned limas, perhaps). There's a page devoted to miscellaneous details of family life: how much their "War Risk" insurance cost, how many shares they had in a building and loan, the date when my grandfather became Fish and Game Warden for Middlesex County, New Jersey—and the date that he lost his left eye to an accident involving a large bird he was trying to corner, reported very matter-of-factly as one more item to accept, record, and remember.

Most of the time, I'm blithely unaware of the presence of this history in my veins; it's forgotten lore that I come from an ultimately untraceable line if you go back far enough with the Huggs and Albertsons and Freedmans and Greenbaums, a line that wends its way back through history to the beginning of things and back to when God first set up these bloodlines and set them free on planet Earth to make their way and do their best and leave some mark along the way.

Sometimes I feel lost in the galaxy among so many cultures, IQs, wars, crazy people, nations, preferences, concepts, expectations, mountainsides, cities, religions, and then I read that I was created in his image and "I am fearfully and wonderfully made" and that this God of the universe, who somehow is present in every moment of history, stoops to be present in my life, my heart, my family tree, and my being. Amazing things come in small packages. I am humbled by my grandmother and her domestic recorded history, which was the beginning of my own beginnings.

I never told her I loved her and never did my relationship with her justice. God gave her to me anyway so I could be a Hugg and maybe someday learn to can a peach without causing ptomaine. I don't know how it will happen someday, but when I give up this life for the next, I hope there are grand reunions and we can all tell each other those things of the heart that really mattered that we never learned to say or do properly this side of the lima beans.

HOLY CUP

On the dresser in the spare room sits a battered Styrofoam cup, with musical notes and a message written on it in ballpoint pen. Louise blessed me with it at a time when I was confused and unclear about what to do, where to move next. Doesn't sound like much of a gift?

Louise was about twenty-five years my senior. I met her when she came to our divorce recovery program at the church where I was a member, and she and I hit it off, along with various others who formed our own little church rat pack, terrorizing the local diner after our meetings, taking trips together, going to retreats together, and helping each other along that recovery path to healing and wholeness by *being* the church for each other, crying and laughing on each other's shoulders, being family for each other. Louise eventually joined the church because of the TLC of our group and the love and grace of God she found there.

In 1985 I was single and not in a good place emotionally, financially, or spiritually, and I had a job offer for less money than I was making at the time. The new job would be at a Christian conference center, and it included an apartment. It was in a town I didn't know, in an area I didn't know—but the work promised to be useful, creative, and interesting—with a free apartment. But it was a huge move, but I wasn't happy where I was living, but the work would be a good learning experience, but I'd have to uproot, try new things, and meet new people.

I was sitting with Louise at a seminar at church that was less than scintillating one Saturday, so we started passing notes to each other like we were in fourth grade. We filled up the little scrap of paper we were passing back and forth with debates over what was the best thing, what were the positives as opposed to the negatives, and my last question to her was something like, "How am I supposed to know what's the right thing to do?"

It looked like my question was the last word on the last blank space on our little paper, and then Louise looked up at our table, picked up her Styrofoam teacup, and wrote on it exactly what I needed to hear, what my heart was afraid to trust in if I was going to make the big move and jump off the cliff and bite the bullet. Louise wrote simply, "God will take care of you," and embellished her musical message with cute musical notes.

My debates and doubts and arguments vanished into thin air with that simple, non-biodegradable, loving cup comment. With it came no guarantees that God was confirming, "This is the way; walk ye in it," or sending me a telegram saying, "Take this job!" but I had so many indications that it *could* be a positive thing—and I knew I was scared of making the change. So if I'd had a heavenly telegram of confirmation, what would I need with faith? And if there are heavenly telegrams, would they look much different that this lipstick-stained cup?

I took the job, the apartment, the challenge. It was a great experience, the best thing I could've done at the time, and God took care of me. Louise and I walked around the campus when the lilacs were blooming a couple of years after the Styrofoam cup message, and we laughed and shared gratitude about where God had brought us, geographically and spiritually, since we had met each other in divorce recovery. God had taken such good care of us both, though the trials we were going through when we first met didn't make us feel like we were under anyone's care. But God knew what he was doing bringing Louise and me together. We *were* his care for each other. That's how he works sometimes.

Walking and talking under the lilacs was to be the last time Louise and I walked together on this earth. The cancer, though we didn't know it at the time, was already taking over her body. Louise was gone before the lilacs bloomed again. She left a quiet, loving legacy behind, passing on the message she had learned from God, that "he will take care of you" all the way through divorce, cancer, etc., and part of how he does that is to use the gift of friendship to give us someone to walk with when we think we're alone.

PROXIMITY TO SOME
KIND OF GREATNESS

I've been within a few feet of some very famous
people. I sat next to Mickey Rooney on the steps of
the Drew University Library one day in the eighties,
and we chatted; he was filming a short-lived television show there. (The other star with him was Dana
Carvey, in his pre-*Saturday Night Live* days. We all
thought he was cute, but no one knew who he was,
so we ignored him for Mickey.) I met Fred Gwynne
(from *The Munsters*) on the same campus, but he was
not as friendly. Ryan O'Neal was doing a movie with
Fred Gwynne at the time; I got his autograph. There
were rumors that Farrah Fawcett was also on campus,
but we never saw her. I saw William Shatner in a play
at the PaperMill Playhouse in New Jersey, which is
not an auspicious claim to star proximity, but it was
fun nonetheless. I saw President Bill Clinton and

Al Gore in speaking engagements—not together—but there was a presence of greatness about them and a sense of where they had stood on the world stage. I watched a *Prairie Home Companion* show and then had the opportunity to meet the very charming Garrison Keillor, who chatted with us afterward and signed his autograph on a playbill in a cold, dark parking lot in Morristown, New Jersey.

I had the privilege of seeing Kevin Spacey in *Moon for the Misbegotten* on Broadway and was dazzled by his presence on stage and at the stage door afterward, where he graciously signed autograph after autograph. I've seen the rock group Genesis, Peter Gabriel, Eric Clapton, Little Feat, Bruce Springsteen, Tom Petty and the Heartbreakers, Billy Joel, and Jethro Tull live on stage. When they emerged on the stage, inundated by the lights and screams of fans, it was with tremendous drama, and inevitably there was a freakish, hands-held-high reception to each one, creepily like a church full of the faithful raising their hands to praise the Lord. The lights and spotlights and the adulation—it was almost obscenely like a church service, in worship to this great entity. We raised our hands and shouted and laughed and sang along to the very familiar songs; they acknowledged our adoration with great thanks and many gestures of love. For a while at each concert, this is pretty obvious and uncomfortable for someone whose deity is not Phil Collins. But after a while, it becomes the norm. I lose myself in the music, a happy part of the massive crowds, partaking of the glitz, wishing I could be closer and reach out to this icon in front of me who is playing the music that has been the backdrop for my life. There is something mystical about these people and groups who have been the musical background of my childhood, teen years and adulthood. They are heroic; they create music that fills the entire stadium and replaces air with light and fantasy. The venues are designed to totally overwhelm the senses: lasers and fireworks, dazzling in the night sky or the dark stadium, the decibel level designed to fall just short of making eardrums bleed, the seething humanity all focused on these beloved creatures on the stage, and usually the smell of some interesting vegetable matter ignited and definitely being inhaled. It is exhilarating and exhausting and wild. It is the definition of idol worship, and it is designed to be overwhelming. I go to hear music I love, but I can't help being drawn in by the mob hysteria.

The USGA (US Golf Association) museum is near where we live. In it are the clubs, winning golf balls, and personal items of everyone who is and was ever anyone in the universe of hitting the little white ball into a hole in the ground as people cheer nearby. I've stood near bits of the golfing lives of Jack Nicklaus, Tiger Woods, Arnold Palmer. I was moved to read the story and see the personal effects of Babe Didrikson-Zaharias and Ben Hogan—both of whom made phenomenal comebacks in the sport after Zaharias's devastating cancer and Hogan's grisly car accident. To be near the clubs and bags that belonged to them was like being near them. Like being in Yankee Stadium in Monument Park. Babe Ruth played across the street from there. (It was a lot more impressive in the actual, original stadium where you could say, "Babe Ruth actually played here," but progress takes its toll.) Mickey Mantle, who *was* baseball when I was growing up, made his career and became a legend in the shadow of this place.

In the coming kingdom, it will be the loving, eternal God we are yelling for and his beloved lead Son and the Spirit on percussion. Earthly, earthy things often point to the divine. Humans can take any good thing and make junk of it. But when I finally arrive and am in the presence of the ever-loving Creator of the universe, I want myself to burst into flames in his true, eternal light. To be in his presence will be an afterlife's permanent occupation. The excitement of the famous and the rock groups I love are only a faint shadow of the wild, raucous joy that is to come.

Apologies to all those who were hoping for peace and quiet and the aforementioned harp music, but I think eternity will rock the heavens.

STORIES OF SNOW

I can't think of much else in my life right now that brings me back to the excitement and joy of rare childhood bliss and innocence than a good weather event—in this case, a blizzard, a good New Jersey nor'easter. In my childhood, the predictions were probably, "There's a big storm coming with lots of snow on the way," whereas now, with our sophisticated meteorological research teams and equipment, we get winter weather advisories and storm alerts to let us know that, well, there's a big storm coming with lots of snow on the way.

During a recent weather extravaganza, as we were snuggling in for a long winter's nap and the storm was beginning to tuck in, Tom was musing about how customarily quiet it gets when the snow is falling and beginning to accumulate—and it was at that moment, like an offstage cue, that the wind started to howl through the eaves and the trees and that front gutter that needs remounting. And all night the wind whistled and sang, like in the movies, and the beagle curled up closer and closer, and I dreamed about being with my parents and being home. I don't remember the plot, but my dream mind was seeking shelter and times past. I woke up early to the clock radio, which sounded like the intercom at the train station with muffled signal, and I didn't need the announcer explaining to me anyway; I got up (a tribute to the excitement of the storm, as this usually takes longer to actually get my body moving) and looked out the window. (By the way, this is the most accurate mode of weather prognostication—meteorologists, note: looking out the window is great for picking up weather clues.) My world was a gigantic wedding cake. Wind was blowing the hissing snow horizontally, and everything was blanketed except my fire-engine-red car, which seemed to have been in a wind-tunnel effect in the middle of the driveway throughout the night and all the snow had blown away from it—the cherry on top of mounds of butter cream snow.

I know that storms like this are dangerous and people get hurt, people go hungry and are desperate, and I don't mean to negate the difficult realities of it.

But the reality I'm referring to is that I am totally isolated with those I love during an event like this, and
my world shrinks to this little pioneer, simple, ride-
out-the-storm existence—with lots of food available,
maybe some movies on television, lots of tea. All of my
concerns and my schedule and concepts for the week
are set aside. I am powerless over the forces outside,
but I am safely sheltered and content. I can't take for
granted today that I am fabulously wealthy to have
a warm, cozy spot and a sufficient stash of food and
water for tea to weather the storm, and I am blessed to
have a loving spouse who wasn't stupid enough to try
to get to work in a blizzard. (We've chatted about this
in pleasant voices many times over the snowy and icy
winter months.) And the storm is gregarious and glorious and fierce in its power, and I am humbled by it and
by this ridiculous sense I often possess that I actually
have control over my destiny, my plans, my days, and
how there is a power in the universe greater than my
ego who is closing down the East Coast of the United
States of America by turning water into pretty, mul-
tifaceted crystals that are falling in great number and
turning the world into a clean, white ice pop.

Is it that I believe in God because I feel powerless and need a crutch? Do I believe because of a feeling of contact, of presence, of some inexplicable tenderness that filled a need? Am I a person of faith because of my study, my reading, my discussions with people great and small? Do I read God into events, coincidences, happenstance to make myself less fearful in the world? Well, yeah, sometimes all of the above. But if you asked that little girl standing in the field among the crunchy grass all those questions, she'd look at you, probably with a sarcastic smirk, and say, "Just *look*." God was always there and here, in the moment, right now. I prefer him in the field and in the otherworldly realm of a good blizzard and not in theological tomes. He's ultimately much easier to track down.

DETOUR

My friend Pat and I like to meet in New York City a couple of times a year. We both live about an hour away by train in opposite directions, and we take the train to Penn Station and track each other down. I've known Pat for almost forty years, which is a really long time for anyone to have put up with me. We like to bumble our way through the New York subway system, finding our way to special events and programs and galleries and chocolate shops and trundling through the mouse maze that is the city while sharing our most recent (or most ancient) life stories. We are both admittedly intimidated by the enormity of the city, and we push ourselves to find things, to figure out ways to get around that don't involve spending our whole weekly paycheck, and to have a blast in the meantime. Sometimes we eat grandly; usually, we wind up at a fast-food trough just to get out of the weather and because we can't seem to find the really cool places when we're looking for them. (We're working on this.) We've seen summer days when one could fry the traditional egg with a little bacon on the sidewalk and no one would even look twice—which, of course, no one does anyway in New York City. We've seen winter days that would freeze a moose in his tracks. On the last trip, we were for some reason in the mood to create spiritual parallels to pretty much everything around us. If anyone else had been with us, it would've driven them to despair, but Pat and I are tough and usually pretty giddy by around noon. We were at the American Museum of Natural History on 34th and had to get back to Penn Station, but the C train wasn't running, so we had to take the A train (yes, that's a song) to 125th uptown so that we could catch the A going back to Penn Station downtown. As we rode, slightly dizzy on chocolate, our life stories were verbally weaving themselves into the complications of the journey (it was a long ride). We have had to go uptown to get downtown, we have had to switch tracks to get back to where we started from, and we measure our progress sometimes from too far away to have hope of home; but we always know we'll get there by the light of this thing called faith. Of course, we arrived at our destination as millions of travelers and commuters do in New York City, but this is a challenge for the two of us, making the effort to do something that's not in our day-to-day suburban routine. We walk by faith, not necessarily by sight in the city.

I try to get home before dark.

GIRL ON THE LEDGE

For a while I wanted, and prayed, to be able to return to the purer faith/religion of my childhood—the one where I connected to the God of the universe through the visuals of nature, the seasons, and the quiet glory of skies with clouds or stars or vivid colors of the world. God likes children's faith, right? I wanted to live more simply with less angst and more joy with abandon. It seemed like a good idea.

But I can't go there anymore. Seeing simply isn't faith, and there's been too much grief under the bridge to set aside all realities to just gaze at nature. I still do gaze and enjoy and revel in the beauty of creation, but it's secondary now to the reality, the power of my adult faith.

To give thanks to God as an adult is a courageous thing. To have been disappointed at how my life has turned out, to be angry at prayers answered with *no*, to watch loved ones die, to hear about wars, political repression in a cruel world, and hunger and homelessness in the American town where I live, and to find gratitude in my heart for the God who is present, who gives me the calling and energy to action, who gives comfort to the world through his children, is, in itself, comforting to me. I can't just wander back to the garden again. I live in a world created for love and beauty that has long since given way to the pollutants of uncaring power drives and desperate longings that find fulfillment in everything but the love of God.

I see unspoiled creation and find joy in it, but God is bigger than the garnish—the background of nature even in all its beauty. God is in the tough stuff— the loss, the pain, the questions that will never find answers in this lifetime. I enjoy a gorgeous sunset, but I more commonly grow and learn and get stronger when I can't see anything.

THIS IS THE DAY THAT THE LORD HATH MADE

I chronically live in every possible frantic moment other than this one—the only one that serves God and reality and is grounded and connected to what really matters—the *now*. I choose to live in tomorrow's dread, yesterday's humiliation, next week's dinner party, thirty years ago when someone left me. I am a worrier, with memories like swarming gnats. And I am fearful of things that will come, bitter about what has gone ages before. And I've lost the sweetness of moment-living, like the child has on the swing as the sun is going down on a long summer day and the world is going quiet and the crickets' concerto takes over the heavy humid air, in time with the rhythmic screech of the old swing chains, and being alone on the swing, feeling the night breeze cool my face and tease my hair, watching the moon rise over the hills is *everything*. Nothing much else exists except my feet reaching for the horizon, the exhilaration of each freefall, the stars beginning to appear. I had my worries as a child, but I was capable of reveling in the moments of God, each one a gift, each one feeling like it would last forever, each one exactly as God must've intended it, personally for me.

My best fitness of faith comes when I am right where I should be, swinging in the summer air, caught up in a moment's call from God to look, to remember without fear, to breathe in, to grasp, to feel, to provide some harmony for the song. This moment, me writing—you reading—these words, is God's moment for us both. God save us from the tangle of the web, the multiple agendas, the dirt-colored glasses.

THIS IS THE DAY TOO

It's here. Sic the dog on it. Go back to sleep, and it will doubtless go away. Throw that inkwell. Sound the general alarm—but not too loudly, please.

It's morning. It's the a.m., when we gleefully leap from our beds singing, "This is the day that the Lord hath made; let us rejoice and be glad in it!" Or not. I prefer the going-back-to-sleep thing. I am not a morning person. I'm more a four-in-the-afternoon person. Certainly not an a.m. person of any sort, unless there is coffee—lots of coffee.

My husband gets up almost every day at 4:15 a.m. He prays, he exercises, he might even jog. Lord only knows; I have never been awake with him to find out. His discipline amazes me; he amazes me, though he will inevitably say it's never good enough. I love my husband. He is the love of my life, the one who has stuck with me, the one God sent when I was really hoping not to have to live alone.

I'm amazed to have a gift like him, someone who still loves me after a lot of years, someone who follows God on the same path with me, who is on the same journey with me and keeps me company through the joy and grief and insanity and fun of it all. I have friends and acquaintances and a brother, cousins and aunts and uncles on the road with me as well. But there's something about a soul mate for me. I always wanted one. I prayed for him. I *could* live without him, but I just never wanted to.

He helps me to find God when I wander, when I'm morose, when I'm too dense to see the cliff in front of me. The days God gives us are full of gifts, which I don't always see.

It's good to have someone to let me know where to look. So this is the day God made. Someone figured that out about three hours before I awoke to it. It's good to have someone to share it with.

GOD IS MAD:
DISCUSS

As I go with that flow they talk about, after having hung out on the planet for fifty plus years—fifty screaming-megalomaniacal-pointy-haired-boss-type-churches-forbidding-me-communion-fuzzy-dice-big-haired-weeping-evangelist-mononucleosis-my-mother-the-car-disco-plastic-fruit-chocolate-covered-ant-telemarketer-Barry-Manilow-Heaven's-Gate-pet-rock-eight-track-Screaming-Yellow-Zonkers-Zen-of-everything-Michael-Jackson-Elvis-lives-God-is-dead-Vietnam-is-merely-a-police-action-Republican-Congress-Britney-Spears-as-role-model-reality-tv-chain-letter-plastic-Jesus-Reaganomics-years—I daresay that the reason we don't get the big questions of life is that we don't understand that the Creator-God of the universe is simply eternally loopy.

Look at these examples. God creates this glorious, perfect world with great technical detail and care and with great love; he declares it good stuff, then he lets the inhabitants, created in his image, pretty much trash the place—beer cans everywhere, holes in the ozone, glaciers melting all over everything. God has something to say to Moses, so he communicates through incendiary shrubbery. He lets this Moses guy wander in the wilderness, never asking directions for forty years with his precious flock—and then he doesn't let the guy go into the land he promised. He tells Hosea to marry a prostitute. He sets off a nuclear bomb on Sodom and Gomorrah and turns a woman into a salt statue. And that's just the Old Testament.

He decides to beam down to earth for his grand entrance to save us and gets himself born in a smelly stable to a dubious young couple who don't even have stock options. He goes to a wedding and doesn't set them up with an opening prayer, sermon, and collection afterward; he just goes in and makes more wine so they can get happy. He has all these great opportunities to set the record straight on why things are the way they are, but instead, he talks in funky, nebulous stories and throws pigeon salesmen out of the Temple. He gives himself up to be killed—lets the bad guys walk right in and take him—and lets himself be the kind of religious sacrifice the Jews have been doing for thousands of years, making himself a pigeon, and then—here's a really cool thing you'd *expect* God to do—he comes back to life. But then he really doesn't tell a lot of people about what just happened and never gets the marketing thing going, and then he goes back home to see what we'll do with it.

He then leaves *us* to represent him—lets *us* invent his church on earth with help from his Spirit—and *then* lets us continue with indulgences, crusades, and forced conversions, then Testamints (little breath mints wrapped in Bible verse wrappers), statues of Jesus playing soccer, bobblehead saints, WWJD bracelets, tattoos, mugs, and Bible covers, the aforementioned big-haired, weeping evangelist types who get hugely rich by saying the name of Jesus a lot and begging money from those who can ill-afford it, and we have so many different denominations of "churches" that no one can tell the difference between the CRCs and the PCAs and the PCUSAs anymore without a multi-volume set of score cards. I know God's in there somewhere, but who would let us do this but a totally crazy God?

This is what I'm saying.

MY BEST MOTHER

When I was eight, my mother was first diagnosed with paranoid schizophrenia and was sent to a state hospital where no one hoping to be cared for or rehabilitated should ever be made to go. And in 1961, electric shock treatment (ECT, electro-convulsive treatment, to be precise) was still no better than a torture-chamber tactic, and no more therapeutic, but there was this dear thirty-three-year-old mother of two children who had an illness no one was even beginning to understand, who was forced to endure six months away from her family (with torturous weekends where she could come home to visit us, and my brother and I would be on our best, albeit well-acted, behavior, and it still wouldn't be enough to make Mom want to come home and live with us and be part of the family again because she just wasn't strong and whole enough yet. In our minds, it was because we weren't good enough to have our family back again yet, and we'd have to try harder next time.) and endure multiple "treatments" of electric shock and medications that may or may not have made her symptoms and enduring side effects much worse. By the time my mother was able to come home to stay with us, her mother—my fifty-six-year-old Hungarian grandmother—had died while Mom was hospitalized, and no one had told her until the funeral was over, hoping to spare her something that ultimately spared her nothing and caused more of her fragile psyche to cave in with amplified grief and bitterness. Her children, meanwhile, were crushed under the weight of attempted goodness that we could never hope to attain to try to make her well, to make her stay home, and her husband was angry and frustrated and blamed for pretty much everything that had happened during the time my mother was away, by everyone, including himself.

I was in fourth grade that year, and my brother was in sixth, and we both have school photos and report cards from that year that neither of us can conjure any memories for, so uncertain and agonized was life for us all at that time. I remember screaming fights in the house. I remember hiding in my brother's and my room with Rusty, our faithful collie, and cowering and listening and plotting schemes to get rid of Mom and Dad, willing to take our chances with the foster care system in New Jersey at the time just to have what might pass for peace. The raging outside our refuge was a terrifying adult world that we loathed and wouldn't fully comprehend for decades.

In 1966 came another blow when Mom was "sick again," sent to another hospital—a real hospital, not just a state institution—where she met a doctor who was to be critical to our family's survival. I never met this doctor, but he found the right medicines at the right time to pull Mom out of her illness in time for my eighth grade graduation, in time for us to all somewhat reconcile and pull some semblance of a family together before my brother took off for college, air force, and then freedom from us. I was thirteen when the miracle doctor appeared, and he stayed with Mom and kept her medicated and well functioning for many years.

My mother, and the family, endured this incredible disease, the death of my grandmother in secret, the relapses of mental illness, which my brother and I took years to fully come to accept wasn't our fault. And where was God during all these years? Weeping with those who weep. Bringing me up himself when my parents were busy in the wars. Sending me care-givers who brought salt and light when I was in the dark. In my middle age and beyond, I have found the love of my life in Christ and am at peace with the past through which he led me, my wilderness, my desert, my whale of a childhood. God didn't stay in the flam-mable shrubbery. He came out, put flesh on the Spirit to console, to give wisdom, to give me the courage to live in that adult world.

BLOOD OF LIFE
AND LOVING
YOUR NEIGHBOR

"I don't like needles." I've heard people say that so often, and it is like saying "I like to eat food," or "I don't like sticking my head in a wood chipper"; it all seems fairly obvious. Perhaps someday medical needles will be like the Star Trek hypospray jet injectors, but for now, needles of the sharp, medical variety usually signal that there is something that's going to happen that's not fun, and you might want to turn your head for just a minute.

But needles are a necessity for saving lives, administering vaccines and painkillers and things that are good for you, things that will cure what ails you. And they also are a channel for blood donations. Though maybe someday, there will be effective faux human blood products, right now, the only way to get this lifesaving substance into someone's veins for surgery or replacement or whatever is needed is through human donations, via needle, from my vein to your vein.

I don't like the feel of a needle, but I donate platelets as often as I can, along with red blood cells. I can donate every three days when donating platelets; it's every fifty-six days for red blood cells or whole blood. In my veins is a miracle, one that can be split up into its various components and transferred directly into another's veins to save a person's life. Platelets go to cancer patients; red blood cells go to those having surgery. Collections are also made of plasma (used for burn victims, as are platelets).

I don't like needles, but I am grateful for good blood pressure, freedom from illness, cooperative veins, and a healthy heart so that I can do this small thing for my neighbor. I spend an hour (for platelets), lying in a comfy couch, watching a movie or reading (one-handed) a magazine or book, listening to this amazing machine that is separating platelets from the rest of my blood (and returning the other blood products to me) so that someone else has a chance to beat whatever trauma his body is going through.

Who is my neighbor? I've never met the recipients of these donations, and only God knows their identities, but each of them carries something of myself, as I carry something of God from his invention of me and his blessings of good health and his infusion of saving blood, the blood of Christ. There are all kinds of analogies for the transfusion of God's life to mine, Christ's being to my being. It is a miracle of life, this blood thing. It makes that momentary pinch of the needle worth everything.

HOMETOWN

I was brought up in a little town called Pompton Plains, part of Pequannock Township in New Jersey. (The names Pequannock and Pompton are American Indian either meaning "a place where they catch soft fish" or "we don't want you to learn to pronounce our name.") Derek Jeter of the New York Yankees was born in Pequannock; if there is another claim to fame there, I haven't heard about it. I was brought there in 1952 to the little house on the former orchard; the house and the orchard are long, long gone. I was brought up on *Lassie*, black-and-white sodas and black-and-white television, hula-hoops, Del Shannon, the end of polio, and all things fifties. It was probably the United States' most idyllic, naïve time, when the middle class of the United States of America thought they ruled the world, kids were still spanked and "seen but not heard" at family gatherings, and you could protect yourself from a nuclear blast by putting your coat over your head. It was a heady if not singularly dim-witted time.

But all those houses with the chintz curtains and collie dogs in the front garden had their secrets and their fears—and a future that included the sixties, seventies, eighties, nineties, zeros—protests, assassinations, disco, Peewee Herman. There was much to fear and innocence to be lost.

Looking back, it seems like the whole country was set in Jell-O, on display on a pretty plate without much substance. Too much sugar and not enough honesty as to what was really going on deep down. The world was in big, big trouble with the threats of the Soviet Union, the KKK at home, nuclear bombs that nations were threatening to throw around like snowballs, and a world war that had left parts of Europe pulverized. Hey, it wasn't my fault; I was just a little kid. But I grew up without ever being told how to actually make my way in the world. It was idyllic, and no one wanted to burst the bubble, to tell the kids life was anything more than pleasantries and good manners as the new eleventh commandment to the good life. If you worked hard and did well at school, life would be your oyster. You could be anything you wanted to be. You would go to college even though your parents were never afforded that advantage. You were privileged and could reach out for the stars. Dreams could come true. Follow your bliss.

Those fabulous fifties gave way to now. I am mostly all grown up, mostly a whole, fulfilled adult having found healing and grace along the multitudes of bumps in the road. Looking at today, I feel overwhelmed by this business of getting older, leaving behind the old days that were a little less complicated (as seen from this side of them), and since they're in the past and complete, they're easily categorized and filed in my memory banks. It's today that's hard. It's living with questions and fears that's the difficult stuff of life. But I am a child of grace; today is God's. Maybe the world of the fifties was the same world as today; people were kind, and people were cruel. The rich got richer, and the poor got poorer. There were and are vicious diseases without cures. The government was loved; the government was loathed. I am not a child of the fifties or sixties; I'm pretty much just up for today. That's all God gives me—plus love, which still seems to be in style. I don't want to think about getting old, living on the pensions and savings, having my freckles turn to age spots. So the fifties were nifty. The places and faces are on file. I'll take today.

HOT SURFACES

I finally bought a new toaster after twenty years. We'd been using a beat-up old toaster oven with food baked on from the previous century (and possibly the century before that), and I finally decided, in a fit of spontaneity and shopper zeal, that I would bust the budget for the week (ten dollars with green points) and buy a plain-Jane, two-slice, white generic toaster to sit on the kitchen counter.

It is a respectable little toaster. It mostly just merrily toasts bread and the occasional bagel—and it amuses me. I like the little sign by the top of the toaster, next to where the slices go. It says "hot surfaces."

What a revelation! All these years I've used toasters, toaster ovens, and the occasional campfire to toast bread, but I never realized that it takes—*heat*! I thank the company who diligently created my little white toaster for alerting me to the "hot surfaces." But alas, it doesn't tell me what to do with the "hot surfaces."

Do I spurn the hot surfaces, thereby avoiding actually making toast, or do I revel in the joys of the "hot surfaces" and warm my hands by their kindness?

Then there are the candles ordered from the Internet. I love these scented candles in particular but never realized they actually came with instructions. For example, prior to lighting the actual candles, one should "remove and discard the packaging." So if I just remove the plastic stuff but don't discard it, something bad will happen? And I am to keep the burning candles from pets, who apparently are flammable. Sid, take note. But nowhere does it say that even as your beagle is singeing his little tail by the flame of the peach-bubblegum-rosewater-strawberry-preserves candle, there are "hot surfaces."

I'm sure there's a lawsuit in there somewhere.

So many instructions in life, but so few when it comes to the stuff I actually need to know, like how to pick out a job that makes sense according to my skills and personality, how to get along with those people in my life who insist on their inherent superiority, and how to forgive, how to love the entirely unlovable among us, how to stop eating vast quantities of chocolate once the chocolate green light has flashed. Our litigious society has created this stampede of utterly stupid "instructions" so businesses can protect themselves. But we could use some real instructions, folks.

I wish someone had taught me to balance a checkbook when I was in high school. I wish someone had sat me down and taught me about relationships with that very opposite sex: the male of the species. I wish there had been instructions when I signed up at age fourteen, explaining that my spiritual life in Christ was not going to be black and white but had eternal shades of gray and purple, and that ghastly things would happen that would be so monumental as to make my head spin around a dozen times and land a block away, and I would have to retrieve it and find a way to reattach it. That's where we need the instructions. I know if I light a candle, rather than curse the darkness, that it will burn the skin off my hand if I try to grab at the flame. I know the bagel I just toasted and the metal bars in the toaster are going to be hot for a while, thanks. But what about the black hole of depression that comes to visit, the deep ache in the back of my throat when I think of my father's loss, the conversations with impossible people I'm faced with over the phone, the chronic resentment against some who chronically marginalize me, don't hear me, can't see who I really am? Where's the tear-off tag that tells me what to do?

The instructions come in putting one foot in front of the other. They come sometimes by sticking my hand in the flame and feeling the heat and finding out that I need to pull my hand away. They come from God, who created the heavens and the earth, and the basic horse sense to keep moving till I find the way out—or in. Or sometimes to sit still and wait for the still small voice of love to tell me what's really happening. The instructions are in the basics, that love is always the bottom line to dealing with any person, that care and compassion and a freedom from self-centeredness stem from that, and they're always a good idea to follow when I don't know what else to do, and that learning to balance my checkbook—or my heart—comes from reaching out for help to someone who knows how. Jesus, the Truth, told me that.

SEEING A ROBIN

I have a contest going with my friend Sue every year: who will see the first robin of the spring? It used to be a contest with my dad, and he would be proud that Sue has taken up the cause, though Sue usually wins. Since robins don't actually migrate anywhere but just sequester themselves in the woods when winter comes, and since Sue skis and hikes and is more out-doorsy than I, she almost always sees that first little red-breasted guy and calls me to gloat. It's good that we're close friends.

But for some reason a couple of years ago, I never actually stopped seeing robins. I saw some in late November, then before Christmas, then during a thaw in January, then during a warm-up in February right before the blizzard. Robins everywhere. It's not much of a spring revelation this year. Nothing much special about seeing a bird.

But I saw a surprise ladybug on the curtain in January after a snowstorm. (My friend Barbara found a baby bat on her living room lace curtain, but that's another story.) There were snowdrops blooming in great profusion by the birdbath under the blizzard's drifts. In early March after an ice/sleet storm, there were crocuses blooming by the back porch, pretty little yellow starbursts—and I don't even remember planting crocuses there.

God sometimes shouts, sometimes whispers, sometimes watches and loves and waits for me to catch up to him. He leaves hints everywhere of his creation, his grace and love and presence. Sometimes he arrives as a friend or a robin or a blizzard. I need to keep watch.

ANOTHER STORY

"Love thy neighbor," the Book says. Give to the "least of these," and help those in need. So when Barbara called me up in despair that there was a small bat hanging around on her living room lace curtain (I don't actually think she has a belfry), I was obliged to go over and assist in some way, wasn't I? Couldn't find a good excuse, anyway ("I'd be scared" just didn't seem adequate since it was hanging from *her* curtain), and my strong, brave and astonishingly handsome husband conveniently wasn't home. (In case there are any future bats, it's his turn.)

It was just a little bat. I was afraid because bats move fast, and this one could fling itself at us and tangle in our hair—isn't that what bats do?—with one swoop; bats can carry diseases (can't they?); and bats don't have a positive reputation in literature, stage, or screen. But bats are God's creatures, and I knew we didn't want to hurt this odd-looking creature tangled in her curtains. The "God's creature" comment is true; the fact is I would've been too wimpy to try to do away with it. So our solution, developed quickly and scientifically, was to somehow get close enough to wrap him/her up in the curtain, thus trapping it, take the curtain down (which meant one of us had our arms wrapped around a bat that was wrapped up in a curtain) and quickly—very quickly—bring the whole package outside to her porch and leave it there until the little one untangled itself and merrily flew back to its batty little family. Or it would flinch as we approached it, and we would both go screaming out of the house like two little five-year-old girls whose brother had just flung a worm at us.

We very slowly approached the curtain from opposite sides. I hastily and efficiently wrapped the two edges of curtain together as she brought the bottom up to wrap it upward. We fumbled with all the edges but managed to make a nice, loose little ball around little Dracula. She got the curtain off the rod with one push. We were out the door in seconds, dumped our little package on a chair, and ran away. It worked! And we watched the little bundle. And we waited. And waited.

She never saw the bat again. When the exterminator came the next day and pulled the curtains aside, there was no one there. We are hoping she/he wriggled out of the top in the night. Maybe not. Maybe the bat still lurks in the house. Great rescue mission.

Friends are gifts when they can share adventures and tears and joys—and small rodents—God's creatures—hanging from curtains. Love your neighbor; you will be grateful to have done so if you ever have a bat curled up in the living room drapes. We're still laughing.

I SEE DEAD PEOPLE

No, I'm not in a Bruce Willis movie. It's just that I seem to go to a lot of funerals. I feel like I'm too young to have been to so many, but obviously I'm not. There have been a lot of big memorial services and small wakes/viewings/services in the small chapel of our church and huge "celebrations of life" in the larger sanctuary with marathon receptions that follow. Sometimes I bake tea breads for the reception; sometimes I am just a spectator and sing the hymns and hear about the person's journey and learn things I didn't know about them. Sometimes I knew them well and hate to see them go. Sometimes I really had no clue of them but just went to a group where they were and felt I should be part of the farewell. Sometimes it's out of family obligation, sometimes church obligation. And sometimes I get blindsided by what I thought I knew about life.

Helen died the day after Thanksgiving. I was really only an acquaintance but always knew she was someone special, and I was honored to be in her circle. She died too young, suddenly, sadly. A glitch in a minor medical procedure became a tragic disaster. The minister created a beautiful celebration of her life and called her the embodiment of Christ's love. She lived fully, died in God's arms. A bagpiper played "Amazing Grace." No one ate my poppy seed bread at the reception. And then the firestorm started.

I met another member of her circle in a department store a few days after the funeral service. "Why Helen?" she asked, and not this *other* person who suffered terribly in pain with so little relief. Another friend cited the substantial contributions our friend had always made to so many, and why "take her out" in the prime of her loving and living and giving and leave some of the dregs behind. (I assume she wasn't referring to me.) And following along with these rhetorical questions to God inevitably came the familiar, tired voice in my own head: "Why did my dad have to die at the age of sixty-eight when some of the crummiest people on earth get to live longer, happier lives?" My brain ultimately defaults to that. Dad was too young; we needed him. I needed him. He took care of our mother for forty plus years; he deserved some happiness, not fear and the nightmare surgery that took his life. He was my buffer against a lot of life and a lot of reality. He had deserved a buffer from the storms himself. He never got it.

From Helen's death to "why did my dad have to go so soon?" there never was and never will be a definitive answer to those questions. I have reconciled over the years with living in the question, having the question like a crevasse in the front yard that I am careful to gingerly step over every day. I've planted flowers around the crevasse, made a pretty little border surrounding it, dressing it up so it doesn't look like the jagged scar it is. But every once in a while, I fall face first into it again. And God is always there to pull me out. No answers. No "Okay, I'll let you in on the secret of this one: your father had to leave the planet on September 8, 1990, because ..." Just him, saying, "I'll walk with you through it; I'll hold your hand while you cry." I can stumble around, demanding answers, or I can fall in his arms and cry my heart out once in a while. The arms and the crying work the best sometimes. And sometimes I see his tears too.

ALL I WANT FOR CHRISTMAS

Ah, Christmas. The smell of chestnuts roasting, Jack Frost and sugar cookies and pine branches and holly— and my frustration at re-gifted Santa kitsch that would choke any self-respecting reindeer. The emotions rising from beloved carols and old wounds and loved ones no longer at their places for Christmas dinner makes me want to hide till January. The pressure to experience Advent and the coming of the Messiah with a broken world while making those cookies at eleven at night because it was the only time I had left makes my brain hurt. There's a weariness that rises in December like no other weariness. It is the rote repetition of tasks, frequently with little recollection of why they continue after the joy has already been spent.

Welcome to Christmas week. Tom and I get together and watch classic Christmas movies with friends who haven't seen them, which is a nice way to start wending our way toward the big *kahuna* of all holidays. We always try to spend a few evenings with friends in December doing something "Christmassy." It makes me think about traditions and my own memories of Christmas and how I would feel a huge loss not to have a big tree with all the ornaments from our travels and from our friends and families and how I would miss the movies and the lights in the neighborhood and even the giant snowman head we have fitted over our outside lantern. It means something to my heart that isn't necessarily connected to the birth of Jesus or really anything to do with my faith, but it's a big part of who I am.

On a recent Christmas afternoon, we followed a fire-engine-red Ferrari Testarossa down the highway toward our Christmas family destination. Even cooler than the car was the fact that the chap driving it was in a gorgeously tailored Santa Claus suit and perfect Santa beard and perfect white mustache. All the cars around us were laden with a backseat full of packages, but his looked empty. Perhaps the whole sled and eight reindeer thing from the night before had so exhausted him that he just wanted to stretch his legs a bit. But there we were, following Santa down Route 287. My already sugar-overdosed brain was a little tripped by this juxtaposition: this is the celebration of the birth of the Messiah, King of kings, Lord of lords and, oh, look, there's Santa in a Testarossa racing down the hill.

I'm always astounded—and this is deeper as I get older—at how quickly the Christmas season and the trappings and the music and the memories are over. But even when it's over, it's coming again. It's a perpetual reminder, despite the trappings and trivialities of the month of December, of the One who came—and will come back—and we will celebrate Advent (his coming) till we get it right. There is always the Christmas whiplash of memories and traditions and trappings versus the true meaning, but if I approach it with the right spirit, I can usually reconcile all of the elements of it peacefully by New Year's.

SNOW SQUALL FILTERED THROUGH BURST OF SUNBEAMS

A rain had fallen from some warmer region in the skies when the cold here below was intense to an extreme. Every drop was frozen wherever it fell in the trees, and clung to the limbs and sprigs as if it had been fastened by hooks of steel. The earth was never more universally covered with snow, and the rain had frozen upon a crust on the surface which shone with the brightness of burnished silver. The icicles on every sprig glowed in all the luster of diamonds. Every tree was a chandelier of cut glass. I have seen a Queen of France with eighteen millions of *livres* of diamonds upon her person and I declare that all the charms of her face and figure added to all the glitter of her jewels did not make an impression on me equal to that presented by every shrub. The whole world was glittering with precious stones.

—from *John Adams*, David McCullough

I do not worship nature, yet I don't think I could've begun or continued a relationship with the Creator of the universe without nature before my thirsty eyes and heart. These are not necessarily in priority order of my love of God's gifts in nature: the scent of lilacs, cardinals in general (though not the baseball franchise), snow at dusk, Vs of geese in an autumn sky, the smell of summer on a wet field, rainbows, the touch of a warm breeze on my arms after a cold spell, ladybugs, the sound of a laughing baby, a beagle getting the *zoomies* (activity named by an employee of the Seeing Eye organization, Morristown, New Jersey, a from-zero-to-sixty racing as fast as possible from one room to another and then back again, risking life and limb and furniture for no discernible reason, until exhaustion triumphs), the crunch of stones in the driveway as Tom drives in after a day at work, cashews, ocean waves, and many, many etcs.

Each morning I have a devotional time when I read sometimes just a few verses of the Bible, and I have a prayer time (although frequently it's interrupted by the dog needing to go out or my brain creating dramatic renditions of arguments where I always win over those who annoy me, etc.), and I do a time of centering prayer, a Christian meditation (except when I fall asleep). I light a candle, speak out loud to God, do everything I can to overcome the fog settled in my brain cells, yet nothing will bring me alongside the heart of God better than the sight of a sky-blue morning glory trumpeting in the garden when there was no evidence that it was going to be there the night before, or the scent of my roses coming to greet me when I sit on the porch on a hot summer day. God's Word is big with the preachers, and I love it, but there's no better practical application of God's loving persuasion than a gentle quivering of new spring leaves in the tree canopy above me in a sweet, warm, early spring breeze.

AND AN ABUNDANCE OF SPRINGTIME

In the Book of Revelation, the Bible says there will be no more tears. There's a shampoo that says that too, but it's not quite as profound. The Bible is talking about an eternal paradise, heaven, forever. There will be mansions/apartments/condos/homes for God's children. Heaven is my home; I want to go there. I miss it; I have a sense of longing for it, though I haven't seen it yet; there are sepia photos of it from the Spirit hidden in my heart. One of our ministers says he won't go there if there aren't dogs. Most of my friends have a lot of questions for when they get there; God apparently has some explaining to do. There's the hymn that says, "Heaven is a wonderful place, full of glory and grace." We all have an idea of the heavenly palaces, the eternal rest, the final perpetual bliss and peace, the cloud nine of secular and sacred literature. Some are nuttier than others.

I personally think Scripture points to all of God's creation being redeemed. The whole of Eden—which lost its caretakers when Eve gave Adam a pomegranate, or something, and Adam blamed her for the fruity fiasco, and they both found out God wasn't kidding about the wages of sin being death—was surrounded and barred by God. Death meant a wretchedly diminished relationship with the Almighty, a boot out of the perfect garden and an end to the physical life of permanent good health, strength, and vitality and the plus of being able to have a walk and have a chat with the God of the universe whenever you wanted to. And it meant populating a planet, which would be full of other living and dying people, and watching them grow old and lose their youth and capacities, which I think is sadder punishment than one's own guaranteed ultimate death. But Jesus came to the planet to bring God's light of love brighter and bigger than anyone had previously been able to elucidate. All creation groans and travails together (Romans 8:22) until that day when he comes back to us. Having prepared a place for us, he will scoop us up in his arms and never let us go again; he will make all things new. He'll take us past the clouds, to another planet (I once heard Billy Graham say he thought that might be God's venue for heaven), or to another dimension, somehow back to Eden where our hearts have always wanted to go whether we knew its name or flavor or scent or not. God will be the light, the music, the last word. We will be changed—we'll have to be to live in Christ's peace with all the other redeemed. There's the old joke about "that group in the corner; they think they're the only ones here." God must groan with his creation.

Some are concerned about boredom. The concept of stage and cartoon is that it will be all about that singing and there will be angels hovering here and there, dipping to the strains of harp music, and St. Peter will stand at the big gate with a massive desk and a massive, dusty ancient volume of names (or perhaps a gigantic Kindle 7), and all those new people coming in every day from heaven-knows-where who I have to deal with will be looking nervously on. There's Gabriel's trumpet—probably waking me up after a long day humming and strumming. And I won't be married, though I quite like being married in this life. Bummer.

I don't know if there are unicorns and pterodactyls and the best prime rib in the universe there, or if I will find I'm wearing ruby slippers when I arrive and am escorted straight to where Dad and all my beloved dogs are. I don't know if we're all reunited with everyone we loved right away, or if it is a giant love-fest as we tear down the categories and earthly titles of family, friends, my people, your people, those people, and we all instantly have the heart to live as one—all creation. I want it to be about bowing before my Creator and adoring and worshiping him—yet he knows my desire to see those I loved on this earth, whom I have been missing and longing for. I know that I crave a quiet place with my God somewhere around the corner from where I am now, and if he is there, and I am free of the web of pain and aging and questions that this planet has to offer, then that will be heaven, and I will be satisfied just to be near the God who is love.

MOVING TO
HIGHER GROUND

When I die, bury me deep; bury my English book at my feet.

Tell my teacher I've gone to rest, and won't be back for the English test.

—Justifiably anonymous

Would someone please proofread the church bulletin for my funeral before it's printed? Here I am, a writer since I was ten, and very fussy about where the commas go, and then someone assembles the final pages that people will ever have to endure of me, and my name will be spelled Judhti—or I'll be called Judy—or something like that. And I'd like cake at the reception—a celebration-type cake of the sort that I haven't allowed myself to eat for years because it's bad for me and might cause ... my death? So at my reception, please no finger sandwiches—no free lunch from me—just a big cake with goopy icing, bowls of chocolate (peanut M&Ms are fine), and nothing that is necessarily conducive to a prolonged, long life. I will be free at that point, and I'd like all the attendees to feel that way too, though not quite as profoundly as I will. They might still be watching those calories, or whatever one is watching that is trendy at that point in time. Too bad.

I would like the 23rd Psalm read by someone who's lived in it, someone who has had his own personal parking place in "the valley of the shadow of death." I want it read not because it's read at virtually every funeral ever staged in the United States but because the Lord really is my Shepherd, and he's held my hand and walked with me beside the still waters, and he has restored my soul and then re-restored it, and then a few years later, anoints my head with oil and heals me and restores me once again.

I want bagpipes, in case there's anyone who's fallen asleep, mostly because if there's an earthly sound that might reach to the heavens, that would be it, and I might catch the sound somehow. And everyone remembers the bagpipes, though they won't necessarily remember me. Sometimes people who really aren't related in any way land at funerals, but there's some unnecessary sense of obligation from a former employer or someone who has to set up the M&Ms, and they may come to my service and not quite be able to place me (I was the gorgeous, size four, sweet redhead with the dimples and violet eyes, by the way), so perhaps at least the bagpipes will give them a short view of heaven and God's grace if I didn't.

Instead of a sermon, homily, eulogy, talk, or devotion by the attendees or clergy, I would like the following: I want Pachelbel's "Canon" and Barber's "Adagio for Strings," as well as "Sheep May Safely Graze" played decently and in order to restore the souls of those present. And if there is someone to sing a solo, "A Simple Song" from Bernstein's "Mass," without breaking the budget (or any windows with a terrible voice, thanks), that would be ideal, though, live or (tacky) recorded, I would like it included in the service. I don't want the congregation to have to sit for too long, so get 'em up and singing "Beneath the Cross of Jesus," hopefully with minds engaged to listen to those words of humility and hope that I loved.

Please don't ask anyone to stand up and opine about my life, unless they're really, really funny.

Please make a program for the service in a lavender color; I'd love a picture of lilacs on the front, which was my grandmother's, my father's, and my favorite flower and scent. Or have a picture of my parents' home, the house where I grew up on Orchard Road. The house I grew up in—not the house that stands now. It will remind people that I'm going to another house where moth and rust and mold will not ruin it, and contractors won't make it new and improved. True design and fashion, I hope, will be eternal.

I'd like for no one to cry, but I am hoping someone will provide tissues just in case. I am going to be so much more happy and secure and comfortable and completely unworried about gray hairs, circulation problems, the price of chicken at FoodVille, and whether the dog has had his fecal flotation done recently. So don't cry. But please take care of the dog.

Tom and I request that our ashes be scattered at Forest Lake, New Hampshire, because it's the one place on earth where we've both found tremendous, profound peace. We figure God can reassemble us from there as easily as anywhere else when the big trumpet sounds. Please, when you open the canisters to scatter the ashes, check which way the wind's blowing. I don't want to go back home in your hair, and I'm guessing you feel similarly.

My "passing" should be in the local paper so no one continues to send Christmas cards or continues to resent me for something I did, perceived or real. The obit should be short and not-too-sweet. And no one needs to see a photo of me when I was eighteen if I die when I'm eighty-seven. I haven't done that much in my life—I just couldn't get all the dreams over the wall—so tell them that I was born in Pompton Plains, died wherever (I am hoping not in New Jersey), whenever, and I was a writer. An itemized list of my various miserable jobs, because writing doesn't pay enough to keep a cat alive, need not be included. I despised most of them anyway. My wooly educational history is also unnecessary to include. The detritus that "everyone loved her sweet disposition" and that I was a swell person and a gentle spirit and made origami birds for everyone can be left out as well. Include details of services of celebration of the resurrection with Christ, time and place. Tell folks to send money in my memory—or not—to feed the hungry or heal the sick somewhere legit and don't get a receipt.

Let them know there will be cake.

I've never been a people person and have never been gifted at expressing what individuals have meant to me, nor have I been able to readily trust that I meant much to them, but my heart worked harder than you can imagine to love and to accept people for who they are and where they are on their journeys—as I hope they accepted me and my foibles, sins, defects, foul temper—and it truly was the best I could do. If I ever told you I loved you, you were loved as faithfully and deeply and loyally as anyone could be on this planet. If I told you I loved you, it probably hurt that I could never tell you the extent of my love. If I didn't tell you, please accept it now. There was never any reason not to love *everyone*. Even you.

I belong to God through his light, Jesus Christ, forever. In Christ, I hope I'll see you there in that place where there are no more tears or pain. I don't know where it is, but it is with God, and that's enough to know. I'll be seeing you, wrapped in his love. Don't miss his grace notes along the way. Over and out.

WHAT DO *YOU* SEE?

QUESTIONS FOR JOURNALING
OR BOOK GROUP DISCUSSION

Suggestion: Be patient with these questions (as you are with all the questions in your life!). If you don't immediately relate to the topic, consider the question from your own point of view and answer accordingly. The point is to peruse your own faith, feelings, and background. Read the Psalm passages out loud if possible; there is a different perspective when the Word is heard!

My Field of Grace; A Place for Me

Is there a beautiful or memorable place you remember from childhood where you first appreciated what God created? Close your eyes and go there in your mind. Take a moment; we'll wait. Write out or draw a picture of what you found and felt there. Read Psalm 19:1–4 out loud and let it sink into your soul.

Raised by Wolves; Deep Waters

How would you describe your upbringing (twenty words or less)? Has your experience of growing up served you well as an adult, or was it something to be overcome? Name one thing—whether you had a fabulous childhood or a painful one—that was missing from your life. If you have children, have you added this missing element to your children's lives? Read Psalm 139:13–17 out loud. How does that compare with your feelings about your own beginnings?

In Touch with My Inner Rodent; A Prayer and a Rescue

Was there an especially beautiful or memorable person (or small furry creature) you recall from childhood who touched your life—for good or bad? Make two lists of the influential people in your life; one list can be a gratitude list, the other can be an "I have forgiven" or "people to forgive before I die" list. Pray through your lists in gratitude, forgiveness, or the willingness to forgive. (Have you included *yourself* on the list of "to be forgiven?") Read Psalm 37:1–3 for some perspective about those who may have hurt you.

Heaven; Gliding toward Pentecost

Draw a picture—or write out a description—of your childhood concept of God. Is there a long white beard involved—or lightning bolts? How has your belief in God changed since you were a child? Is there anything you need to change or let go of? Read Psalm 89:8–13 for one description of God.

Nice View; Dog Byte

Think about your family pet(s) of the past or present. Consider for a moment that the pet was to you what you are to God: beloved creatures who need care, guidance, and feeding from a higher being for survival. Did you ever try to explain to your dog/cat/gerbil not to be afraid of a coming storm or the dark? Whether you had a pet or not, do you feel that sometimes God is "explaining" to you through Scripture and circumstances that he will care for you and not let you fall? What keeps you from "hearing" your heavenly Father's messages? Write out the story of how God has communicated his will and love to you. Read Psalm 89:19–24 for one story of God communicating with his people.

Skies over Budapest; Skywriting

Make a list of places you've traveled—countries or cities or a list of national parks or amusement parks; we each do our traveling differently. Did you find yourself primarily in the mountains, in snow for skiing, or by the water of oceans, lakes, or streams for fishing? What do you find most attractive? What do you feel is the reason for God's creation of beauty in the world? Read Psalm 23—from memory if you can, and out loud— and experience some of that beauty right now.

My Favorite Roof; Showers of Blessings and Tears

From a roof to a child's porch, any place can become holy ground. Picture a man-made place from your childhood or youth where there was a special connection to God, a peace within, a silence that spoke to you. It won't necessarily be a church—maybe a grandparents' barn, a library, a patio on the first day of summer vacation. Tell the story in your journal or group. Read Psalm 46:1–5 for a taste of God's presence.

No Flammable Shrubs in
Sight; Through the Night

Have you verbally introduced someone to your God
and to your Christian beliefs? Write down—or share
with your group—how you expressed it. Have you
had a phase where you had no concept of God or had
a period of time where you could not trust or reach
out to God? At what phase are you with God right
now: a "deep and abiding faith that comes and goes,"
or complete, total trust, or a lot of trust and hope tem-
pered with a lot of pain. Describe—or draw a picture—of a road of faith and where you are on it. Read
Psalm 40:1–4 for a confirmation of God's grace.

The End; Two Hundred Boxes

Which is more detrimental to your serenity in the faith, the quantity of details swallowing up the moments of your life or the overwhelming "big picture" seen on the nightly news, or do these issues not have an effect on your faith? Can faith exist where there is doubt? When have you doubted that God was on your side? What does doubt feel like in the context of your faith life? Read Psalm 130 for a prayer of waiting and hoping.

Write your own psalm of hope.

Moments of October; Having Words with My Mother-in-Law

What were your thoughts about getting older when you were ten? Twenty? Thirty? In what ways have your thoughts changed between your youth and the decade-mark you've most recently attained? What are your fears about aging? Name one thing you don't want to miss! Name one life experience you wish you could erase.

Read Psalm 39:4–7 out loud. Is there something you are still anticipating or hoping for in your life?

Just Routine; Why Me?

The author considers cancer to be a modern-day plague. Read Psalm 18:37–42, substituting "cancer" for "enemies" or "foes." The Psalms can be good fighting songs against illness. Write or talk about those you know who are fighting cancer or some other illness, praying for each one by name. Pray for one who might not have family or friends to pray for him or her.

Remember Me; Wouldn't It Be Nice?

Where does your sense of self and of love come from? Do you identify and value yourself by your job, family name, denominational connections, or the neighborhood in which you live? How did you learn to be who you are; what were your main influences? Draw a stick figure (or self-portrait if you are so inclined) and list beside her/him your primary traits. Check out Psalms 34:1–4, 32:9, and 31:9–11. Do you see yourself in any of these? *Extra Credit:* Can you find yourself anywhere else in the Psalms?

The House on Orchard Road; New Fields

What does the word *home* conjure in your mind? Do you picture your present home, childhood home, eternal home? What feelings are connected with it? Psalm 84 speaks of God's dwelling place—God's home, Zion—where the psalmist longs to be. What do you long for in this life? What is your longing for the next? Does Psalm 84 offer a graspable picture of heaven for you? How about simply Psalm 90:1?

A Chain of Tears; Loose Ends

One chapter is about a prayer chain; the next is a chain of stitches in a scarf. They both lovingly connect the author to people. What's your gift when it comes to connecting with the people God gives you? It could be casseroles shared for a family in need, harmonizing in a choir, visiting someone who has the disease called loneliness. What do you love to do to connect to people? (Read Psalm 18:16–19 for a dramatic connection God makes with us!)

Solemn Records; Holy Cup

Some people save the darndest things! Old farm journals, used Styrofoam cups—what do you have in your attic or somewhere in your home that brings back memories or reminds you of important truths about your life? Photo albums are the easy answer, but what about that flower pressed into your Bible, that Valentine from someone long gone, the necklace from your mother, the child's painting of a tree that looks like Winston Churchill? What story does it tell? God collects tears; read Psalm 56:8. What stories do your tears tell?

Proximity to Some Kind of Greatness; Stories of Snow

What brings you excitement in your life: concerts, roller coasters, chasing tornadoes, a Yankee vs. (insert favorite baseball team name here) game? How would you describe the "high" received from this event? Describe any "spiritual high" moments you've had: walking a labyrinth, hearing the word *benign* after a surgery, seeing your child being born. Look up Psalm 69:30–33 for the benefits of praise. How can you make this cause and effect—praise and shedding its light— more a part of your life?

Detour; Girl on the Ledge

Life takes courage. Being an adult and putting away childish things has not come easily for the author; she would be considered a late bloomer. Read Psalm 73:28. How do you get close to God to be the man or woman he intends? Is there anything in your life you have trouble "taking the big girl/boy pill" about? It could be eating or drinking issues, facing fears, forgiving someone. Write it down; share it in prayer with God and with a single trusted friend or with your group. A good prayer would be Psalm 139:23–24.

This Is the Day That the Lord Hath Made; This Is the Day Too

How do you greet each day? Do you awake like
Psalm 102:3–4 or are you full-blast like Psalm 100?
Fortunately, God loves everyone in both categories.
(A good wake-up prayer to memorize would be
Psalm 143:8.) Write or discuss living in the moment
vs. living in the regrets of the past or fear of the future.
Which do you do more of? Could you spend just one
day when your sole focus is the here and now, the "day
the Lord hath made"? What would that day be like?

God is Mad: Discuss; My Best Mother

Madness is a name we sometimes put to things that are just too much for us; it can refer to that which appears beyond common sense—or that which is diagnosable as actual illness. The acts of God can be dizzying, infuriating, incomprehensible. Psalm 143:3–4 talks about being in a place where God seems hard to reach. Does the title "God is Mad" disturb you? Have you been in that place of confusion and imbalance? How did you find your way back to God's peace? Or if you haven't yet, how do you hope to fulfill that?

Blood of Life and Loving Your Neighbor; Hometown

When the author was born in the 1950s, polio was still a major killer, and many cancers that are curable today were death sentences then. (The good old days, indeed.) Do you view a particular year or decade as being your best of times for you? What were your worst of times? For the bigger picture, read Psalm 78:1–7. Were some of your times of pain also times of spiritual growth? In hindsight, was God's grace present, or did you not sense it? Do you need a "transfusion" of grace in some area of your life?

Hot Surfaces; Seeing a Robin

The Bible has been referred to as an instruction book for life. What is your best lesson from Scripture about living to the fullest; is there a "life verse" that has been your calling card? Read it out loud; is there anything new to be gleaned from it? What does Psalm 37:3–7 say to you today? What have you "seen" of God in your pastures of trust, delight, and commitment lately?

Another Story; I See Dead People

Why do things happen as they do? From the silliness of bats appearing in friends' living rooms to sudden, inexplicable losses, it is difficult to fathom what to make of the small and huge moments of our lives. Is God "in the details," or is he more reserved for the "big picture"? Read out loud Psalm 8:3–9. There is the long and the short of it: God's universe—down to the smallest of aquatic life. What is most important to you today that you need God's help and care with? Articulate it in a prayer, either written or spoken.

All I Want for Christmas; Snow Squall Filtered through Bursts of Sunbeams

Some of the author's favorite things are revealed in these two chapters, and God is in them all. Read Psalm 1:3. What is your favorite season? On one piece of paper, make a chart of the seasons, one for each corner. What memories does each evoke for you? Just write a jumble of words on your page about it. What is it about spring, summer, fall, or winter that brings you joy? Is your favorite season the quietest time of the year for you or the most active? If you write enough, your seasons will all meet in the middle. Where do you see the most of God's work or grace coming through?

And an Abundance of Springtime; Moving to Higher Ground

The Bible pages of Psalms 42 and 43 are the author's most well worn. These two Psalms talk about great disturbance—and great hope. Read them (they're not long!) and consider the age-old discussion of what salvation and heaven will be like in terms of what God is like. How do you picture heaven? Draw or describe it in a journal or to your group.

And before you go: Write up a version of your future funeral plan. (They're often called a "celebration of life," so it doesn't have to be a grim task!) What songs, thoughts, verses would you want to leave behind when you've moved to "higher ground"? What would you want your final witness of faith to be?

BIBLIOGRAPHY

John Le Carré, *The Constant Gardener* (New York: Scribner, 2001), 259.

David McCullough, *John Adams* (New York: Simon & Schuster, 2001), 630.

John Sebastian, vocal performance of "Do You Believe in Magic," by the Lovin' Spoonful, August, 1965, Kama Sutra label.

Brian Wilson, vocal performances of "Wouldn't It Be Nice," "I Get Around," by the Beach Boys, July 18, 1966 and May 11, 1964, Capitol Records.